SHINE
THROUGH
THE **STORM**

Inspiring Stories to Discover
Inner Strength and Balance

Brandi Herdzina

www.BalanceWithBrandi.com

ISBN (print): 979-8-9912638-0-1
ISBN (e-book): 979-8-9912638-1-8

Library of Congress Control Number: 2024918483

Published in the United States by Brandi Herdzina, LLC
Printed in the United States of America

www.BalanceWithBrandi.com /// www.BrandiHerdzina.com

For Mike,

Thank you for the laughter, tears, hugs, unconditional love, disagreements, respect and support, forgiveness, challenges, for dancing in the kitchen, and even for making me giggle toot. Thank you for all of it.

Thank you for our life together.

Contents

SHINE
THROUGH
THE STORM

Balancing All The Parts of You

Fully awake and breathing deeply, I began to feel familiar memories that lived in my bones. Forgotten for a while, they now came like jolts of remembrance—the parts of me that had existed before the life I was now living. Stronger than dreams during a deep slumber and clearer than visions that vanish as quickly as they flash, these echoes of past lives reminded me of who I was.

Breathe, Brandi. Breathe deeply, I imagined. *All the way into the cavity of your belly, through your legs, and out through the soles of your feet.*

The woman guiding my breathwork session was silent, but the bass from the music she was playing reverberated through the floor and into my cells. I could feel it moving me as my body twitched and reacted to the extra oxygen fed to it breath by breath.

Remember. Remember who you are. All the parts of you—from this life and beyond.

* * *

which someone else has painted? And decide what we wish to keep, heal, learn from, and release?

I've spent the past few years doing this work for myself after coming to terms with the knowledge that certain parts of me, when ignored, can have physical consequences that cause health issues. That parts of me could drive uncommon behavioral responses that I didn't recognize as the true me. What I've learned from this work is that unearthing, acknowledging, embracing, and sometimes forgiving those coatings built up over years, decades, and lifetimes of experiences are both necessary and powerfully healing.

Balancing all the parts of me didn't happen overnight. Hell, I work on it consistently to this day! In fact, it will be a lifelong quest to remain present enough, aware and brave enough, to keep my balance and to be kind to myself when I falter. This acceptance has provided me with the wisdom that the quest alone helps me to live a much healthier, more truthful, happier life. That's what I wish to share with you in this book: guidance for how to thrive by discovering the truth about what drives your interactions, your decisions, and your behaviors. Comfort with knowing that this fact-finding search can help you understand what causes you to keep your foot on the gas or hit the brakes. And assurance that this understanding gives you the freedom of choice. That you get to choose how you'll proceed the next time you're faced with an obstacle. And finally, I'll help you learn how to rediscover your balance even if you're the one who created the waves.

I do this through short stories of my own experiences. Each chapter is written from the perspective of a role that I have held or am currently still holding. In each one I capture a day, month, year, decade or more to share what has helped shape who I am today. You'll learn truths about what happened to me, the beauty and misery I have created, the resilience I've found in different circumstances, the mistakes I've made, and ultimately what I've learned from each encounter within those roles that I've held—those roles that have helped make me, me.

At the end of each chapter, I offer space for you to take a turn at uncovering your truths and discovering all the parts that make up the whole you. Perhaps you'll see yourself in my stories, or maybe they will help you discover a forgotten memory that needs to surface. These "Your Turn" sections are meant to guide you as you take the time to unearth your own path forward.

Beyond my short stories and the offerings for your personal discovery, you'll also find inspirational cards for those days when you need a little something extra. Each one holds a special energy that I summoned for their creation. These words, I believe, are not my own but rather were given to me for you. Before writing them, I asked for a download from guides in the highest realm, whose intentions are to serve only the good for all. I asked for their wisdom and words to flow through me for you, following each chapter's lessons and theme. I hope these words and the energy they hold bring you encouragement, cheer, or simply a smile when you need it most.

Like you, I am a regular person living a normal life. There's nothing sensational or different about me, and I think that's the point—that we're all relatively regular, normal, the same, and in this together. That none of us is ever alone in our experiences. I wrote mine down in the hope that this path I've rediscovered for myself and the stories from my life can be a beacon for you to find your own authentic direction. Ultimately, I wrote this book for you and for your family, your team, and your community. For I believe that when we take the time to find our true selves hidden inside and we invite them to the party, we see others more clearly too. It's from this place of clarity that you'll recognize others for who they are at their soul level. And because you will be more balanced, you'll be better equipped to help them open their hearts and invite all the parts of them to the conversation too. I believe this is how we, the regular people, can start to change the world. How we can move away from fear, from unjustified cancel culture, from feeling as though we don't belong or it's "us" against "them." Away from anger, hate, and destruction. It's how we can get back to a place of love for all. How we can get back to respecting Mother Earth and all that she provides. How we can be open and have conversations with one another regardless of how different we may seem on the outside. This is what I believe it will take to bring us back together. We need a balanced you. We need all the parts of you to come forward, be vulnerable, show compassion, and lead with empathy.

And I hope this book helps in your exploration.

SHINE THROUGH THE STORM

Lost Soul
CHAPTER ONE

My laced-up hiking boots hit the hot red dirt of Sedona, Arizona, with anger, hurt, and confusion about who I was after a lifetime of mistakes and missteps. I held such a desire in my heart to leave all those swirling doubts, those racing thoughts about too many "need tos" and "should haves" on that trail and in that sparkling dirt—the Sedona dirt that I'd heard so many say held magical qualities. Feeling headstrong and determined to make change happen, I found a small open space under a twisted tree only moments after starting my hike. It was a sweltering July day, and I didn't feel fully present. I lowered my day pack and sat down with a huff thinking, *Maybe I just need to meditate so I can focus on this hike and be present, for fuck's sake.* I closed my eyes and breathed deeply, but a fly immediately trespassed on my quiet space. Annoyed, I swatted it away, but then four more appeared. As I waved my hands with eyes closed, hell-bent on making the meditation space work, more flies began to appear.

These irritating insects were a physical embodiment of my racing thoughts—bumping into my face, throat, and the back of my head. As they were incessant in their quest to interrupt my desire for quiet, I finally stood up, exasperated, and yelled at them, "FINE! I'M GOING!" And on my way I trekked, heading farther along the trail. But the flies followed, pinging me in the back of the head as if pushing me forward. I was both annoyed at and in awe of this phenomenon. I thought no one would ever believe me if I were to explain it. Then I turned a corner to a piece of the trail that looked like it had been torn from the pages of a storybook—the trees enveloped the path on either side, towering over the sparse but green foliage beneath their canopies. I stopped dead in my tracks as I noticed that the swarm of flies, which only seconds before had been flooding my personal space, were now hovering several feet above my head. Still in a swarm, they hung in the balance high above me, and as I moved forward in the direction of the storybook scene that beckoned, they stayed behind.

Seconds later, a strong wind blew through the trees and all but knocked me over, pushing me towards my left. As I took stock of what had just happened and regained my balance, I looked up at one of the largest trees I'd ever seen outside of the Redwood National Park in California. Towering above me and every other living thing was this petrified tree, gnarled from its life and gray from its death, but still standing strong. As I marveled at its presence, I noticed all of the other smaller trees growing around it and up through the remains of its sacrifice to the earth. Strong though the giant tree was, the smaller new ones now grew in its place.

As I was thinking I might stay in this place forever, and taking a few steps forward along the path to see the tree from another angle, a butterfly appeared on the trail ahead of me. Captured by the beauty of its black-and-gold wings, I was startled when it flew—straight as an arrow—directly toward me. And I froze when it met me face to face, stopping just short of the middle of my forehead before circling around my head to continue its flight back in the direction from which it had come. It was clear my job was to follow, so one foot in front of the other, I obeyed.

We walked, the butterfly and I, for what seemed like an eternity. It was such a long time that I stopped and started to question what I was doing. I thought, *Am I really following a butterfly right now?* But a second after I stopped, the butterfly repeated its earlier move. Again, it met me just shy of the space between my eyebrows, circled around my head, and then continued down the path, as if to say, *Get out of your head and keep following.* So, again I obeyed.

Soon after that, it landed on one of three minuscule red flowers on this otherwise desert-like canyon trail. Having followed for so long, I wasn't sure what to do. *Should I continue walking? Should I stop? What am I supposed to do?* I wondered. As I was contemplating my options and watching the butterfly intently, another gust of wind came through, this time even stronger than the previous one. I steadied my feet and legs to hold strong as it continued to blow through the canyon with purpose. As the wind lifted my hair and attempted to lift my feet, I felt a tingling in my body. Looking down, I saw my hands and arms in flames. I felt no pain as the flames spread and enveloped my entire body. I was on fire, and the wind was still blowing. My body burned to ash, and the remnants of who I had been were swept away with the wind. Chills crept up my spine. Then, as suddenly as the wind had come through, it stopped. I turned in the direction in which my ashes had been swept away and spotted the butterfly once again, hovering over a small clearing before turning and flying away in the direction my ashes had gone.

I felt lighter, different, reborn. For the first time in a long time, I was out of my head and back in my heart space. And I possessed the knowledge within the seat of my soul, within my bones, that a part of me had had to die in order to make room for the new parts of me waiting to be born, to grow.

It was on this soul-searching trip to Sedona that I rediscovered myself and found clarity on why I am here on this planet, at this time. Before that, I had felt completely lost. Whenever anyone had asked me what I would want to do with my life if given the choice to change directions, I stared at them blankly and shrugged my shoulders. The next logical question everyone asked was, "Well, what are your hobbies?"

"Hobbies?" Again, blank stare.

For the majority of my adult life, I'd been determined to pull myself up by my bootstraps, and I'd kept my head down and focused intently on my work as a commercial property manager for two decades. I'd come from meager beginnings so my determination made sense. Growing up in my dad's house it was normal to walk through the garage and past deer being processed, because deer were a source of food for my family. My grandma was always creating new recipes she could make with government cheese. And once, my mom and I were even evicted from a rental house because she couldn't pay the rent.

I knew what life was like without money, and I never wanted to live that way again. So my barometers for success and security were based on paychecks and promotions. Don't get me wrong, in the grand scheme of things, I was blessed. The property management community embraced me when others might have written me off for lack of a college degree. And grateful for the chance I'd been given, I had been committed to making the most out of the opportunity.

Then, as time went by, I could feel an internal conflict growing between the person I was and the person who had embarked on this path all those years before. The woman staring back at me in the mirror had been through some shit, ruffled some feathers, and utterly lost her way. That woman, the one with well-earned wrinkles, had cheated, lied, and was learning what happens to a person physically and mentally when memories and trauma are buried.

I had lost my footing on the path I'd so diligently paved.

The realization didn't happen overnight; rather, it was a gradual awakening. Subtle shifts were occurring that transformed my perception and hinted at the need for change. At first, I fought the larger desire that was building inside me through a few less intimidating life changes. I moved from our centrally located home in the bustling city of Austin, Texas, to a quiet suburb of Denver, Colorado, where horse farms were a short walk from my front door and where I could be in nature more often. I took society's view of a step back in my career, and I created space for personal time and pursuits. After all, I wasn't dissatisfied in my career, only yearning for more fulfillment. But the more I tried to make things fit into the safe version of change, the more they started to fall apart. The company I'd chosen to work for and whose values aligned with mine sold my assigned properties to a new company, which ran its buildings in the way I'd hoped to escape. That, combined with office politics, left me feeling sick to my stomach most days. Managing this while also unexpectedly working with my husband to turn a lemon of a house into a lemonade version of home, and living with friends or in hotels while we did it, often left me feeling like I was drowning. It was as if the Universe was pulling me into an undertow of signs in an attempt to awaken me—to make me aware that I was ignoring my desire to rediscover the essence of who I truly was beneath the layers of career accomplishments and societal expectations.

So, with a mix of apprehension and blind faith, I boldly decided to step away from my job and the successful career I'd worked so hard to achieve. It was a conscious choice, a deliberate pause in a well-established trajectory. Toes over the cliff's edge, so high up I couldn't see the ground below, I leaped, leaving behind the security of a well-paid job, armed only with a faint plan and a hunger for something more. I just didn't know what.

With a little financial planning, I knew I'd be safe to take time off and still be able to provide at least a little support for our family—me, my husband, and our four-legged substitute for a child. Having no plan was one thing, but having no idea how I'd contribute to bills that needed to get paid was something entirely different. Plus, this girl likes to eat! Gone were the days when I could subsist on ramen or feel OK with rummaging for change in the couch cushions to buy dinner. With a slight feeling of security regained, I headed off to Sedona for a solo adventure in search of clarity for what was needed to fill that hole in my chest. Known for being a spiritual mecca and home to energy vortexes, swirling centers for the earth's energy, Sedona offers its visitors a powerful place to connect with The Source. It was this magical connection to the earth's energy that beckoned my soul, which was aching for tranquility, on a quest to hear my intuition. What I found was my calling and my soul's voice, which is part of what led me here to you today, writing this account of my lessons learned.

We all have our contradictions and imperfections. I hope that you'll read the stories of my life and feel connected to me as a kindred soul who steps on toes or trips on her own occasionally. I believe and trust that the self-doubt, fear, and even self-loathing that can appear in the blink of an eye allow me to shine a light in the direction of self-care, self-kindness, and growth.

Each chapter of this book is told from the perspective of a role I have held. Please know that while I've written about each experience from a place of truth, memories can shift over time. Also, I've changed the names of those involved to protect their anonymity.

I start with my experience as a small-town girl, because while my experiences in leadership roles have been impactful, it's my childhood that is the basis for all that I've learned and am learning in this life. However, before we take the first step down that adolescent path, I want to share my belief that before my life even began, I lived others. And from each one I gained knowledge that helped prepare me for who I am and what I'm doing today. My elders didn't teach me about reincarnation; I learned it from people only I could see and the visions or stories they shared.

One of my earliest experiences of reliving a past life's trauma and then understanding later what it was came in the form of a recurring nightmare throughout my childhood. In fact, the nightmare of my entire family burning in a building would haunt my dreams for almost two decades. It wasn't until my early twenties that I learned about past life regression, and in my first session, this experience reappeared. However, this time it felt less like a dream or nightmare and more like recalling a memory—feeling the sensations and stepping into my shoes from a past life. The scenery around me felt familiar, although I didn't recognize it from the life I was currently living. During this regression, I discovered who I had been, what had happened that was causing those nightmares to continuously loop, and forgive myself for not being able to save the living loved ones that had actually been trapped in a burning building. After that, I never had the nightmare again.

Because I grew up in the conservative town of Blanco, Texas, with conservative guardians, this belief that we live different lives over the course of history and throughout the varying galaxies or universes should have been tamped down long ago. Thankfully, it wasn't. Having visions and seeing people others couldn't, hearing their words, and remembering enough of what I saw and heard to ask for guidance from my living elders continued because those experiences and realities weren't squashed. Maybe my family and others didn't always understand these experiences, but they still nurtured them.

My openness to other worlds, ancestors, and past lives grew over time, then dulled, and then reopened itself to me in the mountains of Sedona. Within memories of past lives, I found fuel for the bravery I needed to share this book, this creation, with you. I don't know whether you are a nonbeliever or you believe in God, the Great Spirit, the Source, the Great Mother, the Universe, or whatever you wish to call the energy that I think connects us all, but I am opening up and sharing this piece of me with you. I'm allowing myself to be vulnerable because that energy has welcomed me back and enveloped me in a way that I forgot existed. It has given me the strength I need to move forward and reminded me that balance exists, that we can coexist in harmony, and that it all begins at the individual level.

Over my life of happenstance and through each role I've lived, I was given sometimes gentle and other times brutal lessons in finding the balance we all seek. But because of the wisdom I gained through these experiences, I know that you and I both can find our equilibrium between work, home, shadows, light, and everything in between. Your definition of balance will look and feel different than mine—or anyone else's, for that matter—which is why I cannot hand you a map that will lead you to it. But what I can do is provide you with examples and lessons, of mishaps and mayhem, from my own life that have shown me an imperfect path to a balanced life.

At the end of each chapter, you'll find a "Your Turn" section inviting you to reflect on your own experiences and how they relate to the overarching theme of the corresponding chapter. Interwoven between each chapter you'll also find card-like inspirations intended to provide you with insight, serving as words of encouragement on those days when you need a little guidance or a cheerleader by your side. They are an offering, a connection to where you may be in your life at any given moment. If you choose to use them, here's a suggestion for how to proceed: Hold this book to your chest and ask for the guidance you seek. Then open a page at random. The words your soul needs to hear will be waiting there for you.

From this book, I hope you find inspiration to dive into the roles you play yourself and to uncover the priceless pieces of gold that life has buried in your psyche. I hope there might be some similarities in our experiences that help coax your memories to the surface. And whether those memories are good or bad, I hope that they remind you of your lessons learned. As you journey down the path of your memories, I invite you to join me on the quest for self-forgiveness, the bravery to make amends, and the courage needed to grow into a whole person with both lightness and darkness. Through this growth, may we all find the flexibility to grant others the space to learn from their mistakes as well.

I wish all of this for you so that you can begin to experience life as it happens in full loving presence, reaching for balance between the person you strive to be and the one you are in any given moment.

Let's Begin

The discoveries and lessons in my life continue, and each leads me closer to understanding the nuances of balance. How we flow between shadow and light, and how the time we spend within each brings its own beauty. I believe that when we allow space for imperfection, we find ourselves. And so, as you head into the pages of my life's story, I ask you to consider this about your own life:

What roles do you play?

What opportunities do they provide for you?

What perspectives will allow you the most personal growth?

The map lives within you—
within the seat of your soul.

Be quiet.

Be still.

Go within,
and your intuition will
guide you home.

Small-Town Girl

CHAPTER TWO

I began searching for a balanced life early in my childhood. Although I didn't realize it at the time, I was learning to balance my emotions, needs, and expectations based on the environment in which I was being dropped off on any given day or week. Like many, I am a product of a divorced family. A seventies baby, I was born to parents who were so unalike that they didn't so much drift apart as take speed boats in opposite directions, leaving me swimming in the wake between their departures. As with most first-time parents, they didn't know what they were doing. However, parents in the seventies didn't have the benefit of Google, YouTube, or any other websites to help guide a flailing child through the pangs of separation. Soon after their divorce at the tender age of three, I found myself in the unfamiliar position of having to decide which parent I would spend the weekend with, which house would be considered home, and which birthday or holiday would be committed to memory. I had no idea how to navigate this, but I quickly discovered that if you push down far enough the guilt that comes from choosing one parent over the other, you can continue to put one foot in front of the other.

I have few memories of that time, but I know that I learned to morph my persona, my presence, into whatever the person in front of me needed at any given moment—and most often everyone needed a happy-go-lucky girl. This usually meant ignoring my feelings and placing them aside to control the narrative of what was happening in front of me. *Do you need a smile? I am your jester, your clown. Do you need a shoulder to lean on? I am your rock, and my tiny seven-year-old frame can hold your pain so you can feel better.* I could be hurt, abandoned, or pushed to the side, and yet my capacity for forgiveness was immense, and I was quick to forget.

One quiet morning before another bustling day began, I was sitting on the back porch with my grandma at my grandparents' little white house near the center of Blanco, Texas. I had been living with my grandparents for several months at this point with very few visits from my mom. My tiny body crumpled on the steps of that back porch, I wept while searching for reasons why she didn't want me with her. Doing her best to console me, my grandma encouraged me to try something new with my mom in the future. As she dried my tears, she said, "Baby girl, next time she visits, try to ignore her and we'll see if she comes more often." As an adult looking back, that guidance seems harsh, but surely my tears and feelings of abandonment were clouding her judgment. She had a hysterical child in front of her who often would drop everything to practically throw a parade when her mom would appear. That was easy for me to do. Before each visit, I had long forgotten any hurt I felt after the previous one. That pain would get washed from my memory, and all I wanted to do was rush to her side. Whether it was with my mother or anyone else, I could easily forget any unspoken words that left me feeling depleted and raw. And in return, I would get the gift of the person's time. That was all I wanted: time, specifically with my parents.

Each home, as with each guardian, would bring its own lessons in life, balance, and growth. And as I would come to find upon reflection, my difficult although blessed upbringing—full of love from parents, grandparents, stepparents, aunts and uncles, distant family, and friends—would allow for a multitude of perspectives to permeate my experiences. All of which molded this shapeshifter into who she is today. Looking closely back at each life I lived between birth and age eighteen, I discovered nuanced patterns that explain my habits of today—which I believe might help you spot your own patterns and understand yourself better too. Here are my discoveries.

Unearthing My True Self

Early in my adolescence, my father played the role of protector upon my mother's devastating failure to hold custody. Her unfortunate choice to date and ultimately marry an abusive man raised massive concerns in my family and forced our years-long separation. I have few memories of her second husband, but I do remember that he once physically ripped me from the safety of a small antique school desk chair. That one memory is enough so by and large, I've blocked him from my mind.

At the time, I didn't understand the role my dad was bravely stepping into when he chose to fight for custody. It took years and maturing for me to develop that level of understanding and allow my heart to accept it. Before he was asked to intervene, I knew him as someone who divided his attention as he strove to follow his dreams of being a musician while simultaneously acting as a part-time dad. Those dreams occasionally left me riding alongside him in the van that carried instruments and players for his country and western band. The van had a large, blue-painted wood sign on its side with the band's name, The Middle of the Fiddle. We would travel to honky-tonks in Texas; my job as the band mascot was to change out the eight-track tapes in the van as we made our way to the night's gig. I always looked forward to the cornmeal sprinkled on the floor in those dance halls and how the kids would slide knees-first through it during intermission.

Although I was incredibly shy, I could count on my dad or my uncle guiding me to introduce myself to the kids, and I learned there actually was nothing to fear. I would sit by my uncle's side as he ran the soundboard, until my eyes could no longer stay open. Then he'd make a pallet under the table at his feet for me to lay on and drift off to the sounds of eighties country. To this day, I can pretty much sleep anywhere, and I'm never afraid to introduce myself to someone new.

My father, a child of German heritage born in the post-Depression era, lived a life fueled by finding a way to make things work. Through my young and undeveloped lens, I saw a compassionate man in need of control. His kindness always shone through but it was his desire for that control and my inability to voice my wants or needs that ultimately drove a wedge between us for a short time. Regardless, his voice, sung and spoken, will forever be burned in my heart along with moments we shared, like when we untangled fishing line while he gently talked about the virtues of patience. His words of wisdom taught through the patience of an old soul played a role in teaching me the sometimes messy art of letting go and freeing those we love most.

I learned some hard lessons through our relationship, and some of those are ongoing. Never wanting to disappoint him, I could transform my being into the version I thought he would want to see regardless of whether he asked me to do so. I became so good at hiding the flawed version of myself that for a while when I was older, we struggled to connect like we had done when I was a young child whose filter hadn't yet been developed. Through years of distance and misunderstanding, I had to find my way back to the real me with all the warts and wrinkles without a lot of guidance. Today, while I still struggle with sharing any embarrassing events in my life with him, I feel braver about opening up to him when it comes to what I hold dear or true. And it helps knowing that our disagreements about religion or politics can and do still end with "I love you".

Dad's lessons for me:

- Patience takes awareness and effort.

- Always be kind.

- Create purpose in your work and leave the world a better place.

- Let go and surrender sometimes—it's hard but necessary.

"I wish I could take this pain from you," my grandma would say when I cried on her shoulder about the loss of my parents' attention and what felt to me at the time as the loss of love. Over time, her reminders that other children had no parents at all replaced my pain. I learned how to backfill my less-than-positive feelings with ones of shame and guilt for not carrying the weight of others' pain with me at all times. Yet somewhere along the way, in the jagged contours of that guilt, I also came to learn the truly valuable lesson of how helping others can help us heal. When my tiny toes would stand cautiously at the edge of pity, positive action would shift the energy. More often than not, that action was helping others in our community or going to the nursing home to visit people and bring them some much-needed joy.

When I was about eight years old, my grandma ran a daycare out of her home, and I would sometimes wake up feeling alone, forgotten, and sad. On those days, she would elicit my help with softly rocking the babies to sleep. Something about caring for those babies—so helpless and in need of love—pulled me out of my self-pity. The simple act of creating gentle movement so they could sleep brought me immense calm.

I was and will forever be grateful to know how to move stuck energy from sorrow to relief. However, the missing parts from those valuable lessons were for a long time large pieces that were missing in me. Holes of unknowns buried in my center.

Those cavernous spaces were filled with the feelings and needs that I pushed down until I couldn't remember what they were. True healing began when I collected, through therapy, the knowledge to allow the hurt to surface and boil over, to make its way through the cavity of my throat and out into the world as a voice so punctuated that my life couldn't help but move. The stuck energy transformed. And as life could move, so could that pain. I no longer had to forget the pain by doing good for others; I made space for both to coexist. This was one of the lessons I learned years after I began following the half-truth that she had taught me. The half she knew to teach.

Grandma's lessons for me:

- You can find stability from many sources.

- Listen and feel but don't wallow in negative feelings.

- Helping others can put any bad situation in perspective and even pull you out of depression.

My memories of living with my grandparents off and on throughout my childhood are filled with moments of fishing, waking up to a breakfast of chocolate cake, and dipping my chocolate chip cookies in my grandpa's coffee. (Super unhealthy, I know, but I turned out just fine.) They lived a block from my school, and Grandma would stand in the front yard waiting for me at the end of each school day, watching intently as I skipped home across a vacant lot. Their house was incredibly small, but they somehow created room for me along with my aunt, a teen at the time, who I idolized. The memories of afternoons spent under their watchful eyes making mud pies and searching for doodlebugs bring warmth to my heart even today. Through it all, my grandma played more of a motherly role and I looked to her for stability. She was my security blanket.

My actual mom, who I would cling to between visits, was a fleeting presence in my early childhood. She was in search of her own identity, experiencing and learning from her own choices. As an adult, I can respect that. A product of her own trauma, she was neither ready to be a mom nor the flawless adult everyone was expecting her to be.

Over the years, as I've hit milestones of my own, I've been given the gift of perspective. I've had realizations like, *I am the same age my mom was when she had a sixteen-year-old. And, I'm older than my mom was when I got married.* Seeing the world through the eyes of someone you love can shed light on how you think, or whether you think you deserve to be right. It can even make you question whether "right" is really a thing, or whether some things are just too nuanced to be anything other than just what they are. Later in life I learned that she disappeared to protect me from a man with whom she'd had a relationship that it took years for her to escape. Regardless of reason or perspective, my mom's absence played a huge role in my search for security, an abundance of love, and feeling like I was enough. That search for wholeness has haunted me my entire life and still does to this day.

As I entered my teen years, she would play a larger role. I'd long wanted to know her, to spend real time in her presence and truly connect with the person who had given me life.

During the years of our separation, my mom found her way out of the physically and emotionally abusive relationship with her second husband, but not before they had a child, my beautiful baby sister. Did Mom find the strength to escape on her own, or was she fueled by the need to protect this other little girl? Whatever the motivation, I am proud of her for the bravery it took to break free.

When she moved back to our small hometown and remarried—this was husband number three—I was fourteen and could legally decide who I wanted to live with. After a painful discussion with my dad, resulting in substantial heartbreak, I left the comfort of the home he had created for us to live with my mom, a sister I hardly knew, and a stepfather I didn't know at all. During the next four years, I would find myself in a new environment with someone I barely knew in this life, but who I felt supremely connected to—my mother. It was both tumultuous and spectacular, but ultimately she would rise to the occasion and become one of my biggest champions. My younger self was forgotten and pushed aside by the teenager I'd become for a moment of closeness with my mom. It was worth it and haunted me only occasionally for decades to come.

Mom's lessons for me:

- Be brave, especially when it feels really scary.

- You're right where you're supposed to be.

- Be your own person. You don't need someone else's permission to be who you are.

- Unconditional love doesn't come without baggage, but that kind of love will always be there, no matter what.

The lessons I continue to glean from my parents' presence and absence bring moments of clarity as I see myself mirrored in their decisions. In each passing year, as my age has matched what theirs was when they were facing life's challenges, I've been able to reflect and appreciate why decisions were made. I suspect they live with regrets of leaving the little blonde girl crushed on more than one occasion. We do that as humans. We sometimes come up short. I'm no different, and while I'm learning to embrace my shortcomings I'm aware of, I'm sure I'll uncover more in the next few decades that I'll have to get used to.

Imperfect as I know that I am, I still struggle to allow space for those imperfections. I struggle to give myself the grace that I would show anyone else who makes a mistake. But oh, how big my mistakes have been. The kind that hurt the people you love. And coming to terms with the knowledge that I'm capable of hurting others and myself in the process, in ways big or small, has been difficult. I don't think there's anyone on this planet who wouldn't love to avoid the kinds of missteps that cause you to trample on a loved one's heart, and yet we do it all the time. Finding the balance of knowing I hold both goodness and destruction, of light and shadow, has been an ongoing learning experience.

Your Turn

Think back through the memories of your childhood. If you've blocked out a lot of that time, start small. Where did you play? Where did you lay your head down to sleep at night? How did you feel, and can you discover any themes in the lessons you learned along the way? Can you embrace the moments that brought sorrow or pain, and acknowledge their impact on who you've become while also appreciating the power you hold to release them from your grip and move forward? Immense gratitude and growth can come from acknowledgement and release.

You possess the power to embrace the circumstances you face while holding true to your light.

Strength comes from within, from the light with which you were born.

Dance Team Captain

CHAPTER THREE

I was full of hope and sugar one Friday night during the Texas football season in the fall of 1991, as I prepped and preened before rushing to catch the bus that would chariot my high school drill team to our next performance. Packing efficiently had become as essential a skill as applying lipstick without a mirror. One forgotten item could mean missing the chance to perform and then having 164 high kicks added to practice the following Monday. My mental list hadn't failed me yet, and as I was a teenager, my cocksure approach to life wasn't about to give way to lists or foolproof measures. I'd only once before forgotten bloomers, and while a borrowed pair of clean undie covers for the shortest of short skirts allowed me to dance that night, they did not protect me from the heat that radiated from the blistering pavement as I high-kicked to the sound of our dance team sponsor counting. One does not forget that level of sweating. One also does not forget her bloomers ever again.

Running through my bag, I confirmed that all my necessities for the night were accounted for. Bloomers, of course. Aqua Net hairspray, lipstick, an extra pair of toast-colored hose, gloves,

Vaseline, and my trumpet—which I would need to perform with the marching band, because attending a small school meant doing double duty in extracurricular activities. I was already wearing my uniform: a shiny blue satin skirt hemmed ten inches above the knee, matching long-sleeve leotard, and gold sequin overlay precisely covering my chest with white fringe. I was ready to run.

Learning to Fly

The drill team bus was, in my mind, one of the best places on earth. A carriage for a sisterhood of young women all coming into their own and bound by their common love for dance. The scent of hairspray and the sound of gleeful giggling welcomed me each time I boarded for travel to neighboring small schools, while bright smiles and excitement filled the dark blackish green faux-leather seats. The bus was our chariot, and the ladies it carried were my team and my friends.

We would practice for hours each day, together and separately, preparing each performance as if it would be filmed on national television. There was no fame to be had, not even any Instagram or TikTok back then. We did it for the love of dance and for the girl power that emanated from the field or the gymnasium each time the music started and the first toe was tapped. We showed up for each other. If one person didn't pick up the moves, the whole team couldn't succeed. So, while we might move on to perfect the next eight counts in group practice, there was always a girl or a few girls who would stay late to help until everyone felt good about the routine. This was what I loved most.

As a young girl, I had grown up learning to two-step, the bottoms of my feet clamped lightly on the tops of my dad's. I spent hours torturing my cousins at family reunions trying to coordinate group dances we could all perform for our aunts and uncles. However, it wasn't until the summer before my freshman year in high school that I realized how hard dance could be and fought the perception that my two feet might actually both be lefties. Freeing my body from the control of my mind so I could dance wasn't as easy as I'd expected it to be. But by the grace of God, I secured a spot on the drill team, complete with fourteen girls.

Soon I found myself in the middle of summer dance camp, challenged to memorize minutes-long routines in only one week. Each day we would meet up at the crack of dawn in the cafeteria shared by elementary, middle, and high school students. Ladies only a couple of years older than me would seem so mature and so sure of themselves as they taught choreography eight counts at a time. I can still smell the freshly waxed linoleum floor that my knees would bounce off of repeatedly during those weeklong training camps. I was pressed to learn the art of a fan kick, the correct height of a high kick, and the rhythm of moving hips and head and shoulders in opposite directions. None of it came easily to me, but I wasn't discouraged. In fact, this would be my first true taste of grit.

When the going got tough and I struggled to keep up, I quickly found I wasn't alone. Several newbies on the team were all searching for rhythm, guidance, and really anything that seemed familiar. Through that connection, we discovered a way to help each other through an experience so foreign that our bodies and minds were struggling to come to terms with all the newness being presented at once. Then, we were unexpectedly on the receiving end of kindness and understanding. The young women tasked with teaching us—who, in their senior year, were so much cooler and comfortable in their skin than we were—did not "mean girl" our fawn-like movements. Instead, they showed up like well-adjusted leaders. In those early days, they taught us about the beauty and kindness of reaching out to help others even when someone seemed too afraid to ask.

In these moments, I learned the value of friendship and leadership. I also learned what I was made of and what I could accomplish when I put my mind to it.

For the next year, I followed the dance team officers closely. When they walked onto the floor, I stopped talking and started listening. When they gave critiques, I took notes. I danced in the grocery store's aisles, in the street next to our house, and in the driveways of my fellow teammates. I soaked up all I could before trying out the following year to become an officer myself. And when I became an officer as a sophomore, I didn't stop there. I kept watching, learning, and pushing myself to practice in the small spaces of time between school and homework. I watched MTV videos a friend would occasionally record and share, slowing them down and watching them over and over until I could execute the choreography exactly.

Over three years, I went to officers' camp and learned that more affluent schools just called it camp, for they could afford to send all the dancers on their teams. That didn't intimidate me; it just gave me fuel to try even harder. I would pay attention and learn from the instructors at camp, then bring all I could home to the other girls on the squad. As adults we often doubt ourselves and in doing so we miss out on opportunities for success. We either fail to try all together or we quit before giving ourselves the time needed to succeed. Think about what you could accomplish if you were able to quiet your inner critic and move forward with determination. Because I hadn't yet learned to give my inner critic a voice, over my high school career, I ended up winning awards for precision, team spirit, and original home routine. I was also invited to perform in parades all around the world, and I danced in the Macy's Thanksgiving Day Parade in New York City twice. Although it wasn't my first time traveling outside of my small Texas town (population: 1,200), the trip to New York was my first commercial airline flight.

My first solo experience of seeing the world had come a year earlier, on an all-expenses-paid bus trip to Washington, D.C., after I won a writing contest. That was exciting and fun, but the NYC trip felt different. Both Paris and New York were on my bucket list of places I wanted to experience. Once there, along with hundreds of other National Cheerleading Association cheerleaders and dancers, I would spend hours each day for a week perfecting the routines choreographed for the televised parade. It was electrifying. Then in year two, on Thanksgiving Day, I had the ultimate New York experience. Required to be dressed and on the street ready to perform before the crack of dawn, I jumped, jogged, and stretched to stay warm while hoping that the shivering I felt wasn't the flu. Unlike the first year, this time I would be performing both the larger group routine and one with a smaller group, backing up the actress Lorna Luft with the cameras up close and personal. Maybe it was a stomach bug, maybe it was something I ate, or maybe it was pure nerves, but moments before taking the stage in front of the iconic Macy's entrance, I vomited into a trash can on Thirty-Fourth Street. But I continued on as if nothing had happened. I wasn't about to miss a second of the lifetime experience I was keenly aware was underway.

As I look back on that time of my life, all these opportunities to grow beyond the walls of my small town seem almost magical. I was, after all, a simple small-town girl, but I was unstoppable. Since no one had told me that I couldn't do what I was doing, I never considered any alternative to the life I was creating.

*   *   *

But back to that Friday night in November 1991. All of my practice and determination had brought me there. It was chilly, and the scent of freshly cut grass, Frito pie, and Stetson cologne filled the air. In the Texas Hill Country, the draw of a Friday-night football game was nothing to scoff at. So, under a starlit sky and ten floodlights, townspeople supporting both teams huddled on small wood-and-metal bleachers. Equally as excited to watch the halftime performances as they were the game, the fans screamed and hollered as most of the football players ran off the field midway through the game. The few players that remained ran toward the band and grabbed their instruments to march in unison with their other team.

The band always performed first, giving me the chance to march with trumpet to mouth before handing the instrument off to my bandmate and sprinting to the drill team standing at attention on the sidelines. Playing these dual roles felt as normal to me as waking up to the smell of bacon and coffee. I found my place in the dancers' line under the goalpost and marched knees high and chin up down the outside chalk line to the fifty-yard line, then faced the band, whose members were still standing stiff with instruments held at their chests in the middle of the field.

I blew into my whistle, one long beep followed by five chirps, signaling the miniskirt-topped legs to march onto the grass. Arm in arm at shoulder height, some heads looking left and some right, the dancers took the field. With a left-foot-first pivot, we faced the anticipatory crowd. I breathed in the cold, damp air and felt it warm my upper lip as I exhaled. Quickly, the officers were introduced, and we presented ourselves to the onlookers with a salute, a spin, and a high kick into a jump split. Every time, that split garnered the same wincing groan from the spectators. I was ready to perform, and I was excited for the team to show what we could do together. Each dancer's peripheral vision led synchronized contagions with head pops and gleaming smiles. We moved with arms interlocked, our sparkling blue uniforms connected to create a solid line of kicks all the same height. Perfection. This was what I lived for. A fleeting moment of shining bright with young women who had come together as one to create something beautiful for all to see.

It was often like this during those years I performed with the squad. For a moment, we would bask in the afterglow of the performance before shuffling back onto the bus for the long ride home. The weekend would come and go. We'd do our homework and either relish or avoid spending time with family. But come Monday, we would learn and perfect two new routines. Starting all over again, the squad members would show up for each other and for the love of dance.

Your Turn

Doing something new without the fear of failure can be dangerous and exhilarating. It can also propel your chances of success. We learn the fear of failure over time, and it's often what holds us back or keeps us from trying. Thankfully, I didn't hear words of skepticism until much later in life. So early on, succeeding in a world that others may have viewed as stacked against me seemed doable—I had both the mindset and the determination. For adults who have learned the habit of allowing self doubt to drown out self confidence, finding balance requires the ability to reach deep down for grit while simultaneously shushing the inner critic.

When balancing doubts with what we know we're capable of, it's good to be reminded of the power of believing in ourselves, regardless of the obstacles.

Is there anything in your life you've been wanting to try that could be enriching, but you've been afraid to take the leap? Afraid because you might fall. I encourage you now to give it a shot and remember these words by the poet Erin Hanson from her book *The Poetic Underground #2, Voyage*: "Oh but my darling, what if you fly?"

What if you fly? If no one had ever said you might fall, would you take the leap? Would you try?

Whatever your idea, your creation, your desire—the world needs it now more than ever.

We need you. Now is the time. Plan your steps, then take the leap!

I believe in you.

Waitress
CHAPTER FOUR

"Eighty-six the fish!" the floor manager barked as waiters glided through the kitchen door with stacked plates on their arms and on oversized oval trays. It was 1994, and the Black Eyed Pea was one of a couple restaurants in Kansas City where I was picking up shifts between auditions for acting and modeling work. The decor screamed "Welcome, families!" with its large booths and free baskets of bread, but it was the dark mahogany bar that beckoned the five o'clock crowd for drinks on snowy nights.

Wonderful, that ought to go over really well with the peacock at table seven, I thought after having just taken an order from him for the fish special, and knowing it would be an ordeal to ask him to reorder.

As I filled a small round tray with awkwardly large glasses filled to the brim with Coke and iced tea, the newish manager smacked me on the ass as if to say, "Get to it." Blood boiling, I spun around to face him. Finger to his nose, I warned, "You ever touch me again and you'll draw back a nub." Not giving him time to respond, I grabbed my overfilled tray and rushed out to the floor. I rounded the corner away from the small drink station to the sound of the hostess yelling, "Brandi, get to table twelve! They've been waiting a while!" I turned my head to holler back, "I'm fixin' to. Get off my ass!" and went chest to chest and tray to tray with Andy, a coworker I'd only known for about a month.

Now drenched from chest to toes in the syrupy drinks I'd balanced so carefully on my tray, I was staring vacantly at Andy when I heard a symphony of voices from the kitchen all asking the same question: "Fixin' to?"

"Fixin' to" is a Texas expression used in lieu of "about to," and over the years I've been the butt of many jokes for saying expressions just like that one. Most of the time, I could take a good ribbing and be just fine, but at this moment it became abundantly clear I was going to break down either in tears or the giggles. I was barely holding it together when Andy accused, "Oh my gawd! Why didn't you say you were coming round the corner?"

I burst out into a mixture of tears *and* laughter—a dangerous combination unless the look you're going for is "crazy person." The manager didn't dare say anything, and Andy, in a state of regret for what he'd said, simply gave me a nod to let me know he'd cover my tables for a minute while I collected myself.

In the restroom, I stared at my tear-soaked face in the mirror for what seemed like an eternity. How had I ended up here after planning to go to college, get my degree, and have a thriving career? Gazing into my eyes, I was whisked back to my time on campus at Texas State University, where I'd lived only one year before. I loved school, and studying theater had made it that much better, but given my naive approach to financial planning, lack of communication with my father about how tuition would get paid, and headstrong belief that I should be on my own working as an actress rather than studying about it, my time in college was short-lived. However, at this very moment, I was regretting that decision to leave central Texas for independence in a place that was feeling very much like the middle of nowhere as far as acting was concerned.

Knowing that when I cry my face swells and turns into a bright red patchwork, I decided to divert my attention. This was no time for a pity party or a come-to-Jesus meeting with myself. I turned away from the mirror, looked down at my drenched clothing, and began changing into the extra shirt I always packed in my purse for just such an occasion. Wearing a trayful of syrupy drinks wasn't a common occurrence, but it sure didn't surprise me either. I didn't have a replacement bra, though, and wearing a soaked bra even under a dry shirt was always uncomfortable. Kind of like forgetting to bring flip-flops to the river and then going through the rest of your day with bare feet in soaked sneakers. It makes for a sloshy, sticky mess that results in cold, clammy, wrinkled skin.

And today I would be especially uncomfortable, seeing as how I'd committed to working a double shift and was only half-way through the first one. A schedule with seven doubles in a row, not all at the same restaurant, was leaving me completely exhausted, but at least I'd be able to pay rent and eat something other than ramen noodles for a change. Rest and relaxation would have to wait.

Mostly cleaned up after taking what my grandma would've called a "spit bath" in the ladies' restroom surrounded by customers, I was ready to put a smile on my face and get back out there. It had been ten minutes since I'd left the floor, and already the manager was getting antsy about my tables. He was a short, balding man in his early thirties whose chosen uniform, though not a requirement of the restaurant, was a plaid button-down tucked uncomfortably into khakis one size too small. His nervous energy was anything but desirable to be around, so I ignored him as best I could and went on using my tried-and-true methods of keeping people happy. My nickname at this restaurant was "Bunny," after all. I'd quickly become known for being able to bounce from one spot to the next with contagious happiness. Returning to the floor, I thanked Cristi, a very sweet coworker, for delivering replacements for the drinks I'd spilled, and I promised to make it up to her, but in true Cristi form she wasn't the least bit concerned about that. We'd had each other's back countless times since starting work at this family establishment, and I felt lucky to have found someone I could depend on when needed.

When I arrived at my assigned tables with fresh baskets of bread "on the house," all amount of time that had passed was forgotten. Hell, the customers didn't even notice that I was wearing a completely different shirt. My German aunts had taught me early on that the way to anyone's heart was through their stomach. And I knew that the way to my own heart was through food, so it seemed only natural to share that love.

Serve the bread.

Make them happy.

Simplicity at its finest.

Although this gesture of love was settling the nerves of the guests, mine were still reeling. I longed for some alone time in the walk-in cooler, a huge metal box kept at freezing temperature for meats, dairy, and people who needed to cool off. It was a place so quiet and cold that the sensations and silence could almost instantly catapult me into a different place altogether.

Alas, the cooler would have to wait, along with my desire for rest, as one of my last open tables was filled.

A husband and wife seated in my section by the hostess, looked like they were in their fifties and like they'd stepped out of a Banana Republic ad. I welcomed them as a much-needed break from the party groups and families. The greeting went well, and after a few minutes I returned to take their orders. Grunting when I arrived at their table and refusing to make eye contact with me, the man seemed a bit prickly, but I'd worked with much worse. As always, I offered to take the woman's order first. As the lady opened her mouth to speak, I heard a much deeper voice. Her husband had spoken over her to place his order. Not knowing what to do and figuring it wasn't my place to say anything, I simply turned my attention to the man and started writing on an empty slip of the green-and-white striped ticket book. "Garlic penne pasta, but hold the garlic," he commanded.

"OK, we can do that," I responded, and turned back towards his wife. From behind me I heard, "No. Garlic."

Turning to face the man again, I repeated in a reassuring tone, "No garlic. Not a problem, sir." Turning for a third time to take the woman's order, I couldn't believe it when I heard him say condescendingly once more, "Do you understand? I do *not* want garlic."

Everything went white. And then I heard myself say, "Extra. Garlic. Got it."

As soon as the words left my mouth, I heard a snap and thought, *What was that?* Was it that dickhead manager over-hearing my well-timed sarcasm (which so rarely happened that anyone within earshot should have been proud) and ordering me into the kitchen? Or was it my insides snapping after the day I'd had?

Then it happened again. As I scanned the tables in my section, my attention homed in on a rather large family of eight that had been seated. The patriarch of the group was snapping his fingers. At me! *What the fuck! Am I a dog?* On a roll, I spun around and all but yelled, "Sir, I will be with you in a minute. Knock that shit off."

My nerves had officially jumped off the edge at which they had stood only moments before.

I finished taking the woman's order, who had politely waited while her husband perfected his *How to Be an Asshole* one-man show. Thankfully, my remark had left him speechless. I could've sworn I even saw the woman stifle a snicker.

Knowing I needed to make Snappy Snapperton wait for a while just to teach him a lesson in patience, I weighed my options about which table to attend to first. The new parents desperately trying to console their screaming baby while his toddler brothers smashed French fries into the creases of the booth? *Hard pass*, I thought, and felt a small chill run up my spine as if someone had just walked over my grave.

How about the four ladies who only moments before had been toasting and laughing, but were now shaking their empty glasses in my direction? As I contemplated my options, I jumped at the touch of the manager's hand on my shoulder. Apologetically, he told me that I'd need to cover the tables in the section next to mine. Andy had been called home for an emergency.

Holy Jesus, I thought. I needed this job, so the option of wadding up my apron and chucking it at the manager while ceremoniously walking out wasn't an option—though the fantasy of it was quite delectable. I just wanted to disappear. Or at the very least, slam a hand down on the table with the toddlers and bellow, "*Enough!*" in the best mom-voice I could muster.

Shit wasn't just falling apart; it was flying all over the goddamn place and sticking to the walls. This was officially a shitshow of a day.

In one of the first real-life moments that would teach me a lesson about shifting perspective and energy, I walked off the floor to the walk-in cooler. If I didn't make any tips that afternoon, so be it. There in the cold solitude of the metal box, surrounded by frozen meats and veggies, I took a deep breath. And then another and another. I remembered how I had stood up for myself earlier with the manager, and mentally gave myself a pat on the back. There wasn't a human resources number to call or social media platforms to out him on, but I took solace in knowing I'd left him shaking in his boots, at least for a minute. I took a few more breaths and felt time slow down.

Walking back out onto the floor, I went straight to the bar. "Pitcher of mimosas please," I told the bartender. He looked at me suspiciously and winked. I tilted my head and returned his wink with a smirk. "Not for me," I said. "Not yet anyway."

Gliding by the hostess stand, I grabbed some coloring sets, then set the pitcher of mimosas in the middle of the lively ladies' four-top, wishing them well on their girls' day. My next stop was the family of six. I was surprised by the look the parents gave me when I set down the coloring sets. There was so much gratitude in their eyes, it was as if I had given them free babysitting services for life.

The Snapper, having turned redder with each passing moment, huffed at me when I finally arrived at their table. I opted to kill them with kindness, and the moment that I smiled at the woman sitting next to him, I noticed her give a sheepish one in return. I took that as an apology for the patronizing actions of the burly man in the plaid shirt, as well as a silent plea to not do anything unsavory to their food. Not that the five-second rule for the man's rib eye hadn't crossed my mind; I just didn't think he was worth the bad karma.

I had simultaneously calmed my own nerves and won the matches at each table's Hunger Games. Knowing it would be at least a few minutes until the orders I'd put into the kitchen were ready, I stepped outside. Brittney, an older woman I'd worked with every Friday for months, was standing by the dumpster in the freezing cold, wearing no more than a red polo shirt and light khaki pants without so much as a shiver or a goosebump. We weren't incredibly close, but I'd come to appreciate her rank at the restaurant. Unlike the others who worked there, she was calm and collected at all times, having the presence of a house mother but without any of the warm fuzzies or welcoming vibes.

I knew to keep my distance from her when she was on a break, so I stepped off to the side and closed my eyes. I was surprised when I heard her voice: "I overheard what you told Jared. If he comes near you again, or any of the others, let me know and I'll handle it." With her magnetic brown eyes, Brittney looked at me intensely, and I knew instantly she meant business. She'd been working at the restaurant since it had opened ten years earlier, so I understood this wasn't an effort to posture.

"Thank you," I replied.

Then she walked over to me and added, "It's impressive that you stood up to him. But are you OK?"

I felt the flood of tears return, and as mad as I was by their insistence to come out, there was nothing I could do to stop them. Then I felt the softest of touches on my upper arm—the perfect unspoken physical acknowledgment that said, *I know you need space, but you aren't alone.* Pulling it together, I looked up at this woman who was at least four inches taller than me and smiled. Squeezing my hand, she headed back to the door to go inside, but before leaving she said, "Remember, you never know what kind of day someone has had before they got seated in your section."

At that moment, I realized that I'd let my own experiences earlier in the day cloud my judgment and behavior. I was reacting rather than creating action. I'd always taken pride in being able to change someone's outlook or attitude through kindness. If any customers were having a shitty day, they'd leave my section happier and ready to spread love to others wherever they went next. So I had to ask myself who I wanted to be for the rest of the day.

Walking back inside to the hallway, which housed crates of cornbread mix, brooms, and buckets, I could hear the dishwashers chatting and laughing. I waved to them as I picked up the pace, heading towards the line to see if my orders were ready. The cooks shot me "the look," a simple nonverbal cue that told me they were plating up the orders and that they sure would like something to drink. Take care of the people who take care of you, I've always thought. So I fixed them all glasses of their favorite beverages and set them in the window in exchange for platefuls of food.

Having wind back in my sails, I popped the thirty-six-inch tray full of plates up above my head as I proceeded to the floor to deliver the meals. But this time, I wasn't faking a smile or kindness. I'd found it again in the back alley next to a dumpster. And it was then that I learned I could always find myself, the real Brandi, just about anywhere, no matter how lost I might feel in the moment.

"Ma'am, here's your Cobb salad. Your garlic penne pasta, sir." With a wink I let the husband know that I was kidding about the garlic, and he even gifted me with a small smile. *That's a win*, I thought, and on to the next table I went.

Your Turn

Being overwhelmed not only creates chaos or confusion; it can pull us out of alignment with who we hope to be. And it breeds itself, looking to create more and more tornado-like moments in our lives. In moments of feeling overwhelmed, it's important to invite a sense of calm to your nervous system. If that means shocking your system so it can quiet the noise happening around you, as I did in the walk-in cooler, so be it. However, finding calm can be as simple as taking several long, deep breaths and focusing intently on how that breath feels on the skin and in the body. Once your nervous system is regulated, then creating awareness to watch for signs or angels—the words and wisdom they bring—can point you back towards your true north. Brittney was my angel that day, and although I'd never seen her in that light before, she appeared at just the right time with just the right words to help me find my way again.

There are angels in disguise
all around us.

Do you see them?

Do you hear them?

Open your heart and
welcome their guidance, for
their words and their light
may just lead you home.

Right to where you
need to be.

Trigger Warning for Survivor Chapter

The following chapter (five) is about my experience with sexual assault.

If you are not ready to read about this kind of incident, please skip to the next chapter.

Survivor

CHAPTER FIVE

First I had to remember. I knew something was blocking me. That there was an emptiness, a hole, a moment within me that was frozen and was preventing me from fully feeling. I'd spent a lifetime numbing and self-sabotaging. Even within my twenty-year marriage, I couldn't fully open up and be vulnerable. My husband would ask for what he needed in our relationship—closeness, sex, intimacy. And when he would, I would freeze. It's like my mind would go blank when he asked, "What do you want? What turns you on?" I had no idea—or worse, I was afraid to even think about it. I'd promise to try harder at creating intimate moments so our sex life wasn't all one-sided, but I would fail each time. Making lists, creating calendar reminders for myself to initiate connection, setting alarms to awaken from my hiding were all Band-Aids that could never fully cover the wound I was too afraid to heal. I was perpetually guarded, and as much as I longed to face it, I couldn't.

Until I could.

The healing started with remembering that I had been raped at a party when I was fifteen years old and a virgin.

It took marriage and being committed to someone other than myself to force me to face some hard truths. Here I was, living with a man who had no problem expressing his needs or wants, and I either would shut down or have to drink too much alcohol to access that same kind of inhibition. I read books, and I talked with friends, seeking some validation that I wasn't abnormal, but most often I felt like I was broken— like something was wrong with me. Finally, I decided to try therapy, hoping I'd discover the guidance I was failing to find elsewhere. It wasn't a quick fix, though. I went through several therapists, each one offering a different approach. I found that I could manipulate conversations with all of them. I was a goddamn genius at steering the topic in any direction I wanted, so I didn't really have to talk about myself and this thing that I was terrified might be true.

Over the course of several years and attempts with different therapists, I came to realize that something had happened. I knew the truth, but I still questioned my memory. *Did it? Did it really happen? Or was it all in my head?* I second-guessed everything my body was telling me, because I couldn't recall the details. My brain had protected me from them for so long, they were removed from the areas of my mind that I was able to access. But my body knew. Anytime something remotely sexually explicit or violent would happen on TV or in a movie, I would recoil, getting chills as my whole body clenched, preparing for the worst. I couldn't watch these scenes without having a physical reaction. I still can't. Anytime my husband would share or express explicit desires, I would freeze. Losing my words and ability to interact or play with the man I'd chosen to spend my life with, I would retreat and deflect. There's discomfort, and then there's what would happen to me. It felt as if someone had tied my arms by my sides and slapped duct tape over my mouth. My heart would race, and as I wanted to hide, my brain would protect me by removing me from my physical self. I've since learned that this is called dissociation.

In 2021, during a fight with my husband about intimacy and vulnerability as well as yet another struggle with myself, feeling like I couldn't move but not understanding why, I decided to do something about it. The little experience I'd had with therapy hadn't been effective, so I was reluctant to return, until that marital confrontation ended with a plea for me to get help. It was clear I had to do it for real this time—no hiding, no manipulating, and no lying to myself or the therapist.

I decided to look into therapists covered by my insurance, and I believe that divine intervention led me to the woman I decided to put my trust in. Although she was young, her specialty in trauma drew me in. Still, I wasn't entirely sure she was experienced enough to push me beyond what was comfortable. The main lesson I'd learned from the therapists I'd previously worked with was that I could easily manipulate conversations. My tried-and-true method was to sidestep, joke, or turn the tables and talk about the other person's life in an attempt to avoid discomfort.

I followed my intuition that I should at least meet her, and we had a short introductory call. Finally fed up with my forged attempts to figure out what had happened to me, I asked, "Are you strong enough to call me on my shit in real time?" She insisted she was, and agreed to hold me accountable even when I tried to hide. Soon she was introducing me to EMDR therapy.

According to the EMDR Institute's website (emdr.com), Eye Movement Desensitization and Reprocessing is a psychotherapy that facilitates the accessing and processing of traumatic memories and other adverse life experiences to bring them to an adaptive resolution. In my words, EMDR helps you finally take back control of the scary shit that your brain is "protecting" you from, so you can start to heal.

In the beginning (and I assume this is how most people start), we did some prep work before diving into my intention for being there. I had several sessions to prepare me for what was to come, how to deal with the things that might surface, and what to do when my brain continued to reconcile memories when I was back home. To build trust in the approach to treatment, I first processed some less traumatic childhood experiences. Then, knowing how it worked, I was ready to address the main reason I stepped into therapy. However, nothing could have prepared me for how quickly I would be able to tap into the deep underbelly of my mind.

My very first session tied to the sexual assault brought immediate results. With the EMDR buzzers in my hands (or "shake weights," as my husband aptly named them), the images immediately flashed before my eyes. I was there. The man's hand around my throat as I was held down came like a flash from nowhere. I dropped the buzzers and gasped for air.

My therapist was there; I was safe in the room with her. We worked through the image and panic I had just experienced again (and for the first time). Tears fell, and the release of fear overtook my every cell. Full-body chills and uncontrollable weeping began. I wasn't crazy after all. I wasn't making this up in my head. This had happened.

With her help, I pulled myself together. "Do you want to keep going?" she asked. And as scary as it was, I did. I was there to face this truth and to finally not feel like a deer in headlights when sensuality, intimacy, or vulnerability came into play. I'd love to say the first session was the hardest, but it wasn't. Many were brutal. Each time that I would return to her office, place those shake weights in my hands, and close my eyes to experience what had happened to me, new images, sensations, bracing, nausea, fear, and anger would surface.

With each session, I saw the extreme violence. I felt the raw anger and hate that had been thrown at me at such a tender age. Memories flooded back as though they were behind a gauze curtain, cloudy but visible. I had been drunk for the first time. I had seen porn for the first time. I had been flirtatious and tried to act more experienced than I truly was. Then came the bedroom, where things went too far, too fast. And whether I said "no" or "stop" or simply pushed and fought to get him off of me, he didn't stop. He held me down as he assaulted me and choked me while he called me a tease and whispered that he'd teach me a lesson. The images of that room, that bed, and the blood brought familiar shocks back to my system, shocks that finally had a reason for existence. I had disappeared from my body for a moment in time, and when I walked out of the house where it happened, I still wasn't free. A piece of me would continue to exist in that moment for over three decades.

Sadness and anger surfaced afterward. Why hadn't I spoken up? Why had I been in that situation to begin with? Was I to blame, since I'd flirted and pretended to have seen porn before? Where the hell had my parents been?

Through the resurfacing memories, I had to admit the lies I'd told myself and others, including my parents, in an effort to hide. To survive. I had to accept that I'd done what I felt necessary to keep my body and soul together at a time and in a place that are very different from today.

Over six or seven months, I relived the traumatic experience from beginning to end, over and over, in those EMDR sessions, letting it unfold as I held the buzzing paddles and trusted they would successfully rewire my brain. And eventually the images, convulsions of pain, bracing, and sadness finally eased.

And through those sessions, in my mind's eye, I found Her— that frightened, tiny, young girl—and held Her in my arms. I listened to what She needed and allowed Her to speak up. After all that time, those thirty-two years, She finally had a voice. Together, we worked to find peace and the bravery needed to face what had happened to us. We worked and succeeded at being able to own our shame and embarrassment for having felt free, flirty, open, and curious. She forgave me for keeping her silenced for so long, and I was able to forgive Her/myself for not listening to intuition, for being naive, and for innocently flirting as a fifteen-year-old. My/Her beauty had not been the cause of hurt and destruction. Rather, I finally saw that my life could be beautiful again. I also was able to forgive my adult self for having so much judgment and contempt for that teenager's curiosity. And what I left with was a desire to give that girl, whose innocence had been taken, a safe place to live within my heart, free of judgment and the encouragement to dance, to be courageous, and to let go.

As I made my way through this healing process, and shortly after, I would second-guess myself occasionally. Questioning my memories, I would try and reason myself out of it. *I didn't retreat or become a shell of myself after that event. I didn't give up drinking. On the contrary, I went in the other direction. I drank too much, and I was promiscuous. Surely, women who have been raped do not act in this way.*

For the record, women who have experienced this type of event respond differently. There is no cookie-cutter way to respond to trauma. But when you're trying to find a way out instead of through the emotion, you'll create any excuse. I know; I'm a pro at it. I am grateful for my therapist's help in guiding me through those moments as my brain was working to reprogram itself based on my desire to heal rather than its desire to protect. While I may never have the same kind of comfort being vulnerable with my sexuality that some other women my age have, I now know where the fear originates from, how to feel it, and how to keep moving forward without a shovel in hand to bury those emotions.

I am a survivor of sexual assault, and I am proud to say that I bravely continue to heal.

Your Turn

Finding the courage to face those dark truths has been transformative for me in my quest to discover balance in life. And since processing this truth, I've been able to face other difficult ones and feel much more like a whole person. I am now a couple of years into my healing process and continue to learn as I go. However, two important pieces of information have come to light for me that might help you if you have undergone trauma:

- If you often find yourself saying, "What's wrong with me?" try switching the language to "What happened to me?" Our bodies know more than we give them credit for, and listening to their physical cues can be difficult and scary, but also incredibly healing. You can learn more about this approach in the book *What Happened To You,* by Oprah Winfrey and Dr. Bruce Perry, M.D., Ph. D.

- Should you discover that you experienced trauma and choose to face it, once you've acknowledged the truth of what happened to you, your grief will go through all of the stages and end with wanting to find meaning. Maybe for me, that meaning is in this book. But it was only through therapy that I found the courage and the words to write it.

I do hope that if you are feeling broken or ashamed, you know that you aren't alone. There are so many of us, and there are people waiting to help if you want to get through it.

You've been through the
fire, and ashes lie at your
feet. You choose not to step
over or around them, but
rather through them.

Picking up the pieces of
yourself in the dusty
fragments of your memory
invites strength to your soul.

You've transformed. You can
do anything, because you,
my love, have walked
through the fire.

Actress
CHAPTER SIX

I took a swing at acting and a little modeling in the early 1990s, when most models were much skinnier than some are today. I considered plus-size modeling, but back then I wasn't thin or thick—just close enough to the middle to miss the mark on many a casting director's list of needed characteristics. Still, I was taking my shot, because I had been dreaming of acting and dancing for as long as I could remember, and I was hell-bent on making it, whatever that meant. Sure, on some days I felt more confident than others, but if I didn't at least try, I might never have forgiven myself.

I went through rejection after rejection, and the auditions were beginning to bleed into each other. I was too short, too tall, too curvy, not curvy enough. I wasn't sure whether to try to starve myself or go whole-hog on barbecue. I knew damned well which one would make me less cranky, but which one would assure more work was a complete mystery. And as a young woman, barely twenty years of age, I still bore the innocence of not knowing who I really was, with only a vague idea of who I wanted to be. So when various casting agents gave their unsolicited feedback on my looks, I took it to heart. I held their opinions in such high regard that I would yo-yo from size to size, hoping that one version of me would be liked. Maybe even loved.

One day, after searching the paper for auditions yet again (there were no internet casting sites back then), I found a casting call for a small part. The ad read something like: "Cattle Call: Minor role for [some shampoo brand] commercial." Ugh, I hated that term, *cattle call.* Yuck. But I wasn't incredibly picky at the time.

As I pulled up to a weathered single-story retail center for the audition, I didn't even notice the questionable location or shabby building exterior. A cattle call meant I would be walking into a room full of other twentysomething actresses who looked strikingly similar—all blonde, all bearing expressions of desperation and hunger.

Running a little late as usual, I threw my car into park, hurriedly grabbed my headshot and purse, and then slammed the door of my red Toyota Celica shut. Barreling through the door to the soulless building, I nearly trampled a young woman who could've easily passed as my sister. I put my name on the list and handed over my headshot with résumé to the disinterested woman keeping the auditions from becoming a disorganized mess. Then I proceeded to watch as forty of the same but different young women walked into the side office with their brightest smiles, to perform their best sultry rendition of Meg Ryan's diner scene in *When Harry Met Sally.* In case you've never seen the movie, Meg's character fakes an orgasm—highly realistically. It seemed like an odd scene to perform for a shampoo commercial audition, but who was I to question the producers' motives?

A couple of hours and Lord knows how many fake orgasms later, I was on my way out the door wondering if I'd been remotely convincing. Tossing my oversized Goodwill-find purse into the passenger seat and trying desperately to protect any uncovered skin from touching the hot-as-hell fake leather seats, I put the key in the ignition.

What the...? What now? Please don't tell me.... No! I don't have time for car trouble!

I tried the key again, and again it wouldn't budge. Pulling the key out of the ignition, I closed my eyes and let out an exasperated sigh. When I opened my eyes again, I noticed that the dash wasn't nearly as dusty as I remembered it being. Looking to the right, I saw that the Whataburger bag I'd left on the floorboard was missing. In fact, the car was clean! Like, really clean.

Where are my headshots? I wondered. *Have I been robbed?! Why would thieves clean the car for me? Had it been that embarrassingly dirty?*

As the neurons fired, I started to see other minor differences between this car and my own. The stick shift had a different knob. The door panel was fake wood instead of black plastic.

Holy shit, this isn't my car!

I grabbed my purse and keys, got out, and then gingerly closed and locked the door. Scanning the parking lot, I saw KitKat, my sweet little rundown Celica, one row over from where I stood. Curious, I stuck the key in the door keyhole of the stranger's car and turned it to the left. Yep, it worked. Locking the door once more, I glanced to see if anyone was watching and then moseyed over to KitKat. Once inside, where the mess felt comforting and familiar, I dropped my face into my hands and shook my head. Laughing, I started the car, this time with no issue, and headed back to my apartment.

Sometimes in my life—as in most people's lives, probably—haste has distracted my attention. Sometimes I've even put myself in danger for failing to recognize what was happening around me. But it wouldn't occur to me until I was well into my forties how this lack of attention was so much bigger than any of the moments like I'd had with my Celica that day. I now know that paying attention to surroundings is an act of presence. And our surroundings are one small part of what we connect to when we're present. What signs have you missed by simply allowing hurried daily diversions to pull you from presence?

Discovering Authenticity and My Voice

Back at home that day of the Celica incident, I checked my messages on the telephone's tape recorder while changing clothes to go for a run. The tape made a squealing noise as it rewound to the beginning.

"Brandi, this is your mama. Give me a call and let me know you're alive, OK? Love yooooou!"

"Hi Brandi, this is Barb. I sent your tape over to a group for an audition. It isn't a big part, but it is for a commercial. They want to see you today, so call me..."

Shit! When did that come through? I wondered. *It's still early enough, I hope.*

Barb was my agent, although maybe not a great one. Her hair always thrown up in a messy top knot; she was consistently scattered and running from one meeting to the next. And occasionally she would call me with an audition for a small part. Her office looked like I imagined her brain would be organized: stacks upon stacks of scripts and headshots, none of which were filed in cabinets or seemingly kept in any kind of order.

I called Barb back and breathed a sigh of relief when she said my time slot wasn't for another hour. I wouldn't have time for a run, but at least I had time to shower and look presentable. Understanding that they were looking for the wholesome type, I blow-dried my long hair straight and paired a conservative shirt with blue jeans. Looking in the mirror, I gave myself a little pep talk.

"So you didn't have the sides to memorize in advance. You've done cold reads before, and you can do it again. Chin up, boobs out.... You've got this." Then I flashed a big cheeky grin, shrugged, and left the house.

This is promising, I thought as I pulled into the small parking lot downtown. An older, well-maintained office building greeted me and my Celica. Walking into the conference room, I found myself alone and scared, with no other twentysomething blonde women to hide behind. *What if I'm not good enough again?* I thought. But then I took a breath and walked up to the casting agents as if I'd been in this exact situation a million times.

I had brought a headshot with me but saw they were already holding a copy as I reached to shake their hands across the long conference room table. A tall, lanky fellow with horn-rimmed glasses and dark cuffed jeans looked me up and down as he took my hand. Knowing this was part of the job, and trained to let go of feeling uncomfortable with this kind of brazen inspection, I giggled nervously and said, "It's so nice to meet y'all."

A woman seated on the opposite side of the table looked up from the headshot she was examining and said disdainfully, "Oh. You look just like your picture."

Normally, I would have completely frozen at such a comment, one that was meant to demean or belittle. My brain often failed me when someone was intentionally abrupt. I was always so worried about leaving a bad impression or being rude in return that I think it set the stage for my mind to go blank when I needed a suitable response. Except for this time. My give-a-shit got up and went, leaving me with just the right words to say.

With a crooked smile, I slowly removed my hand from the gentleman's grip while glancing in the woman's direction and deadpanned, "Well of course I do. Who else would I look like?"

Finally, and out of nowhere, I just didn't care if they liked me, and I didn't care if I got the part. I walked out of the audition having read cold like a pro and feeling confident that if I didn't get the role, it wouldn't matter in the grand scheme of things. I knew the next audition would come, and the next, and the next. And in between them all, I would be fine being just who I was.

The next day, to my surprise, I got a callback. Then I landed the lead. The commercial was for an insurance company.

Was this the missing link? Not giving a rat's ass about what others thought? I wondered. Did I just need to let it all go and be willing to walk away if the person on the other side of the table didn't recognize my worth? Being indifferent to what others thought about me might just give me the strength to keep going down whatever path I chose.

On the day of the commercial shoot, there seemed to be a million and one people running about. Cameras were set up beside a car parked in front of a nightclub. A few chairs had been set up for those leading the shoot, and snacks and drinks were out on a table for all to enjoy. I'd brought a few clubwear clothing options, as instructed. Since I was still in my early twenties, this was an easy task. Those outfits were front and center in my closet.

I donned black leggings, a leather jacket, and heels, and then the makeup artist and hairstylist worked their magic while I ran through my lines. Butterflies flitted around my stomach. Soon I was called to my mark: the driver's seat of that parked car. As I gripped the steering wheel, the strangest thing occurred. The butterflies dissipated. It was as if my body knew this was what I was supposed to do in life, and as a reward for doing it, every ounce of me found complete calm. As the day wore on and several takes were shot, I learned that when you love what you do, it rarely feels like work.

Your Turn

Feeling like we're enough comes and goes throughout life regardless of age. Many of us have that recurring struggle to feel like we are enough, we're good enough, or we have enough. Regardless of self-affirmation sticky notes on the mirror, there are just times that we seek and pray for the attention and approval of others. Usually it's a signal that we need to seek out professional help to sort through and unlearn lessons from our formative years. It's also a signal that something internal is out of balance. And typically that imbalance is anchored by a disconnect to the Universe, our intuition, and our inner voice.

When I was an actress, I often wondered if I could be the right person for the role—if I was enough. And I'm still working on not thinking like this today! Do you ever find yourself wondering if what you're working on is good enough, or if *you* are enough? Consider journaling those thoughts and then writing a response in the voice of a parent or best friend about how to positively redirect those feelings. It might help you course-correct, as it does for me when I'm sliding back into old patterns.

Authenticity is not created from the opinions of others. Your truth is uniquely crafted by your experiences and is yours alone.

Let go of other people's opinions and expectations. They're not yours to hold.

Reflect instead on the pieces of your story that resonate in your heart. Then invite them to stay.

For this is the real you.

Retail Store Manager
CHAPTER SEVEN

A radio DJ, taking a break from spinning records to plug some diamond jewelry, cooed into his microphone, "The holidays are such a joyous time of year."

Being a woman, rummaging her way through her mid twenties, I found this to be incredibly irritating. As the smooth talker rambled on, I barked: "Unless you're a retail manager, asshole!"

On a normal day, I would have taken a closer look at why I'd had such a visceral reaction to a run-of-the-mill holiday radio ad, but on this particular day, navigating my car through a parking lot that was a sea of lollygagging shoppers was taking every inch of patience I had. With only three weeks left to shop before Christmas, the hordes of friends, parents, girlfriends, boyfriends, husbands, wives, sisters, and daughters were scrambling to find the perfect last-minute gift. My shift at the women's clothing store where I worked as a manager—one small shop in a big mall—was supposed to begin in less than fifteen minutes. However, at the pace it was taking for me to simply park, I wasn't entirely sure I'd be lucky enough to get there before closing time. Finally, giving up on the dream of finding a spot close to the front door, where I wouldn't have to walk for miles at the end of the night, I homed in on a family of eight loading up in their minivan. As I waited impatiently for their less-than-desirable piece of asphalt, I figured something was better than nothing.

As I put the car in park, I closed my eyes and took a couple of breaths. Grabbing my bag of necessities (heels, deodorant, snacks, a book of affirmations), I bolted from the car and speed-walked toward the many metal double doors beckoning me from below the giant Cheesecake Factory sign.

I actually did love the first few minutes after walking into the mall during the holiday season, especially when I opened the store in the mornings before another soul arrived. At least in the morning, there was a certain familiar smell—an empty, clean scent with undertones of escalator rubber and floor cleaner permeating the overly wide halls. It swept over the tile floors and through the makeshift lounges as a warm welcome to those who entered its cavernous shell before children beckoned, before swarms of people and all of their bodily odors arrived. It was peaceful. Quiet. These were the moments before each store would blast its chosen holiday music soundtrack, before I would swing open the metal roll-up door to the store where I worked, and before I would drag the oversized metal sign advertising sale items to the store's entrance.

While entering the mall in the middle of the afternoon was a bit more chaotic, I was still greeted by the piped sounds of "Last Christmas" and the manic yet cheerful scene happening at Santa's workshop. Something about the familiarity of this daily welcome into the workplace was comforting, and at least for a moment, it settled my nerves.

As I walked through one of the oversized openings to the store on this particular afternoon, I chose to ignore the mounds of two-for-one sweaters wadded up on tables that greeted the masses. I put blinders on as I walked past the half-hung blouses suspended from racks and rounders, the circular, freestanding garment racks we often used in the middle of the store. Well-trained in the art of disregarding madness and mayhem, my eyes tractor-beamed onto the storeroom door as I sashayed my way through children manically spinning rounders and hiding beneath them while mothers, in a state of self-preservation, pretended not to notice. After too many holidays spent in the company of desperate shoppers, my senses had dulled to these chaotic scenes. As one of the store's managers, I had to bring calm to the chaos, direct the team in an organized effort to boost sales, and ensure that corporate's direction was followed when it came to merchandising. But for now, at this moment, I chose to ignore all of those requirements and sprint to our haven in the back.

In the back of the house, as it had always been referred to, there was an odd combination of energies. On any given day, you could find the following in the manager's office: a jumble of papers strewn about the desk, a phone that blinked red with messages beckoning anyone's attention, a half-eaten lunch, and a copy of the "lookbook"—a multipage glossy magazine of directions providing insight into the newest fashions expected to arrive each season and the requirements for how the corporate office expected the floor to flow.

In the main area of the back of the house, at least during the holiday season, was a stockpile of boxes that seemed to breed nightly—most of them ripped open as if a wild animal had stormed the area in search of food. The room was a war zone of plastic-wrapped garments tossed here and there until they could be unwrapped, steamed, and hung or folded for the floor. And finally, there was the bathroom, which doubled as a place of respite. When things on the floor went haywire and it looked like an employee might go completely postal on a customer, this was where that person could go to disappear. It was quiet and soundproof. Here, we could throw toilet paper rolls at the walls, and we could scream or cry until we'd gotten the demons out of our system and felt once again human enough to return to the rest of the world. The bathroom was our safe place.

As I arrived for my shift, I slung my coat and bag on a hook in the manager's office and changed out my sneakers for heels before grabbing a headset and walking out to the floor. The typical handoff consisted of a rundown from one manager to the next about losses (theft), UPTs (units per transaction), and personnel (who had called in sick). The clipboard of info was passed like a baton in a relay race, and the outgoing manager would all but sprint to the back of the house before she or he could be asked to stay longer to cover for any given employee who had called in sick.

Surveying the surroundings, I noticed that there were five team members at the registers, four at the dressing rooms, none on the floor restocking or tidying up, and one at the front who had a skip in her step, as she was very close to finishing the construction of the window display update. This was the third update that corporate had required since Thanksgiving, and each took nearly five hours to construct.

I called everyone together to quickly discuss responsibilities. If there was any hope of leaving before one o'clock in the morning, I knew we needed to start redirecting efforts to refolding, reshaping, and restocking the floor. And come hell or high water, I was determined to do so, because my next shift started at seven a.m. the next day.

As the group of team members in their late teens and early twenties disbanded from the makeshift meeting area in the middle of the store, a young couple sauntered through the doors with an empty stroller and their untethered toddler. They seemed less than concerned about the head start their little boy had on them, and looked only slightly remorseful as the boy plowed like Godzilla through the freshly built store window display.

I ran to the front of the store, arms waving and voice pleading, "Noooooooooo!" My coworker Jasmine stood motionless, mouth gaping. She had spent the better part of her shift carefully hanging fishing lines from the ceiling to dangle miniature disco balls, and wrapping empty display boxes with shimmering paper that would reflect the dazzling prism from the lights above. In a matter of seconds, that gleeful little boy destroyed every last detail she had painstakingly constructed. The front window looked less like a Fifth Avenue holiday window display and more like the average American living room following the frenzy of gift opening on Christmas morning. With hours of work now demolished, Jasmine's shoulders slumped in defeat. As her nose turned pink and her eyes welled, she turned on one foot and without a word headed to the bathroom. No one had to ask.

It was pointless to share in my coworker's frustration, as surely I would have my own before the night was through. Instead, I assured the couple that all was well and to enjoy their shopping experience, offering to hold the stroller at the front unless, of course, they wanted to give their little boy a break from being on his feet. They obliged and placed the screaming little Tasmanian Devil into his temporary restraint.

Reassigning the window girl to the back of the house, where she could sort through boxes and prep clothes for the floor was the most humane thing I could do, so over the headset I made a quick shift of responsibilities, and everyone confirmed they understood. "Ten f'roar," I said into the headset, giggling in the hope that it might lighten the mood.

Finally, the daily lull set in, and the afternoon crew, grateful for the break from fake smiles and attempts to kindly offer a larger size because "that garment is running small for some reason," started the required floor move. Yes, with a new window display generally came a requirement to revamp the layout of the sales floor. Surely it was to boost sales of a certain item that the company had made too many of, but in the middle of December, it just seemed like cruelty. This move thankfully didn't involve the whole store; however, moving sweaters that hung along the back wall and folding them for the shelves at the front would take some effort. Together we would have to rebuild the shelving to match the updated lookbook requirement and fold all of the sweaters into neat little rectangles.

Our team worked together quickly, but since the store was absent of windows to the outside, those of us on this crew had no idea night was falling until the next wave of employees showed up for their nightshift to begin. Breaking from the focus of the task at hand, I welcomed the new faces to their shift and helped transition the guard from those who were leaving to those who were taking over. With the new crew in place, I headed to the back office for a quick snack break. Sipping some tea and crunching baby carrots, I reluctantly checked the voicemail.

A wave of dread, anger, and defeat swept over me as I heard the panicked voice of our regional manager—who, in a chipper tone, would usually run through numbers meant to inspire.

"Hey team, this is Karen. I um, I have some *great* news! Um, your store has been chosen as the check-in point for the executive team's tour of Texas! Yay? The vice president of sales and the director of merchandising want to see *your* store. How great is that? So, um, they'll arrive tomorrow at eight a.m. I'll be there too. I know I don't have to say that the new layout needs to be fully in place and spotless before they arrive. So, um, see you *tomorrow!*"

"What the actual fuck?" fell from my lips as I slammed down the receiver.

Of all the bullshit calls to receive, this one seemed like the biggest hit. How the fuck was I supposed to pull this off? Had

Karen really just called and tried to make that news sound like a win for us? Had she really just called and not shown up to help?

Knowing I needed more hands to pull this off, I started making calls to plead for help. Starting with those I knew were the fastest and most adept at floor changes, I picked up the receiver and called the first of many. A few "I already have plans" and "No thank you" responses later, I had all of two extra people to help out. I wasn't surprised. I'd waited too long to check the voicemail, and now it was impossibly short notice. I hated calling the other managers, knowing they were each already scheduled to work almost eighty hours that week, but I was desperate. Thankfully, on the first call, I got a yes from Hannah.

Hannah was a workhorse, though at first glance you never would have known it. She was only five foot two inches tall and wiry, with auburn hair and bright green eyes. But she had laser-like focus. Once she put her mind to something, it got done. And fast.

Knowing that I'd lucked out by getting Hannah's help, I rallied the troops at the register and shared the news of the next morning's surprise visit. Giving space for the grumbling, I dug deep to find my inner cheerleader and reassured them that it was all doable. Careful to not make the same mistake our regional manager had made, I stopped short of trying to convince them that this visit was good for the store or them individually. That would have just felt fake. Instead, I promised to personally reward them with Cinnabon and pizza that evening while they all worked.

Everyone, myself included, felt a new sense of possibility and hope as we set out to our assigned floor positions. Together we continued to work on the lookbook changes until we were inevitably pulled away by a shopper or distracted by children needing supervision while parents rummaged through tables of newly folded sweaters, pants, and tees. We made progress, even if slowly.

Then the evening rush happened, and all of our progress was quickly undone. We all realized it was a futile effort to keep anything remotely folded or prepared for a corporate visit. Even the sweaters folded neatly with tissue stuffed in their middles (a trick used to fluff up the woven threads) were yanked from the highest shelves. We all watched in disbelief as tissue paper fell gently to the floor. It was our busiest night of the season, and sales were hitting an all-time high. There was no chance for anyone to work further on the lookbook updates. Even the people who had graciously offered to come in and help specifically for that purpose had to exile themselves to the back of the house. There, they set up a makeshift area to fold and prepare garments that would later be taken out after the doors had been shut.

Finally, the last shopper was escorted out as the doors were lifted to allow her to exit. And then the doors slammed shut. The sound of the metal door rattling its way closed brought a sigh of relief. We looked around at the destroyed floor, then at each other. As if someone had released nitrous oxide into the air, every single one of us began to giggle. The giggles turned to snorts, which turned to belly laughs, and soon we were weeping at the sight: a mountainous mess that had to be meticulously cleaned up before the light of day. It was ten fifteen p.m.

As promised, I had ordered pizza in advance, and knowing it would be a long night ahead regardless of whether we took a break, I encouraged everyone to grab something to eat and to get off their feet for a bit. Sitting in a circle gossiping about the crazy things we'd witnessed that night and sharing a meal, we filled our bellies and refilled our souls. At that moment, I realized it was community that we craved, and fashion just happened to bring us together.

By sharing this moment, we experienced a renewed sense of energy. We were ready to get to gettin', so each one of us took a station and began reorganizing the holiday-hurricane aftermath.

I cranked the sound system to nineties pop music. As if we were one organism, this team which just happened to be all women on this particular night, moved in sync and flowed through the task at hand effortlessly. In two hours, we miraculously cleaned up the catastrophic mess and finished the lookbook floor change. Dusted and mopped, the floor sparkled. Tinsel hung from high, and miniature disco balls spun from the ceiling. Twinkling lights danced along the tops of perfectly displayed angora sweaters and empty boxes wrapped for show. As we stood at the front looking in, we felt accomplished. It wasn't a miracle; it was women coming together and putting in the work to get it done.

We grabbed our bags, turned off the music and the lights, rolled up the door, and walked out together. Sure, some of us would return in less than seven hours to do it all over again, but for now, we were on top.

Your Turn

Whether you're managing a retail store or leading a campaign for world change, the resilience of your team is paramount, and your ability to lead effectively through chaos is necessary for their success and yours. How do you overcome obstacles and find moments of joy in even the toughest situations? Being clear about this before you hit speed bumps will help guide you on the dark days. The key to bringing team members together so that all support each other is creating a sense of community. Lean in, ask for help, and be honest—be real with your team, your squad, your community. Trust that they'll have your back, and in return, have theirs. It takes a village to get through the tough times and it takes preparation to lead a team toward balance.

You're on the right path, and it's time to shine for your community—for the collective whole.

Invite peace and joy into the spaces of your heart. Here, you'll find calm within the chaos. And together, you'll find the strength to carry on.

They whispered...

Call on me.
Call on me.
You are never alone.

Medical Patient
CHAPTER EIGHT

By around 2006, I had been working as a massage therapist
for a couple of years, and I loved the opportunity to help
people while integrating my spiritual nature into my work.
In massage school, I had gained an understanding of how the
body's tissues can hold tight to memories and emotions, and
how everything is interconnected. Through the classes, the
instructors prepared us for various situations and educated us
on the intricacies of anatomy. I learned many crucial lessons,
but the most important was how to safeguard my energy while
facilitating healing.

The teachers gave all the students guidelines to create an
energetic protection for themselves. I found my version in a
visualization exercise that I performed before entering any
place I would be working at. Closing my eyes and breathing
deeply into my belly, I would picture a bubble of light surrounding my whole body after emanating from the center of my chest
or beaming down from above. I imagined protection from the
outside world, as if I were sitting inside a snow globe. In this
calm state, I could operate freely without worrying about anything permeating my personal space unless I allowed it.

I religiously practiced this meditation before any massage I gave, until one day when I was running late for an appointment with Ren, a gentle soul and a regular client. I simply forgot.

Nothing about this session was unique, and I began his massage like any other, with a few cleansing breaths. As I proceeded through the massage, however, I felt unfamiliar waves of energy. Goosebumps ran up my spine, and the hair on my forearms stood up as if I'd just walked outside on a thirty-degree day. Signaling the end of the face-down work, I placed my hands on Ren's feet. As I touched his soles, I felt mine plant into the floor in a way I had never experienced before. Suddenly, I felt grounded, bracing for something—though I wasn't sure what. And just like that, Ren started to cry. A flood of tears fell from his eyes as he released a pain that ran so deep, he no longer recognized it.

After giving him some space and time, I asked if he wanted me to continue the massage, and he signaled yes through his faint tears. Using slow, sweeping motions to help move his surfacing energy and emotions, I felt his presence become lighter. After ending his session, I stayed only long enough to recommend that he spend some time doing anything rooted in self-care.

Leaving his place, I headed home and proceeded with my nightly routine. However, as I was getting ready for bed, I noticed an unusual pain in my right hand—an ache that seemed to generate heat and a pulse from deep inside my bones. I shrugged it off as exhaustion or a strained muscle, put some ice on it, and went to bed.

Unfortunately, the next morning I woke to a very angry rash on my face, back, and upper legs. My mind was racing as I replayed every moment from the day before. It was all mundane and repetitive until I got to that last massage. At that moment, I realized that I had forgotten to perform my protective bubble exercise before walking into Ren's home—his energetic space.

Calling out to my husband, I was terrified of what this meant. Had I absorbed the negative energy that I'd helped Ren process the day before? Was I physically experiencing the emotional pain that had surfaced for him? It all seemed so far-fetched, and yet nothing else made sense. I needed a realist's perspective, and just then, my husband arrived by my side. He comforted me, saying that I was likely just having an allergic reaction to something I'd eaten or drunk, and he left to get me some Benadryl. Offering to call the doctor, he kissed me and encouraged me to rest.

I soon got in to see my primary care physician. The first of what would be many doctors, this general practitioner rushed through his examination of me, a seemingly healthy thirty-two-year-old woman. First, he failed to see any connection to the knee surgery I'd recovered from a couple of months before this visit. Then he all but rolled his eyes when I walked him through the massage and energetic exchange that I felt sure had some connection to this strange and sudden shift in my health. Within fifteen minutes, he had decided I was having an allergic reaction and recommended I see an allergist. I felt defeated, unseen, and ignored. Frustrated about the lack of answers, I made an appointment with an allergist while also seeking out other avenues.

The rash continued and morphed, as days turned into weeks and then into months. Each day brought new ailments. Lumps popped up under my skin, rashes appeared on different places of my body only to disappear like shadows at sunrise, and jolts of pain sporadically shot through me, sometimes in the most peculiar places. In the beginning, all of this was very difficult to explain, and as the days went by, the pain increased.

Flare-ups would come and go. I'd have occasional relief followed by painful attacks, each one worse than the last. When I had moments of peace, I dove into research to try to find answers, but to no avail. For about a year, I moved from one medical doctor to the next, along with acupuncturists, a Reiki practitioner, nutritionists, and nontraditional healers that my friends lovingly nicknamed "witch doctors." I spit on cotton balls and sent in my saliva for testing, lay still breathing slowly while acupuncture needles only angered the inflammation, and lost twenty pounds on an elimination diet guided by a doctor and a nutritionist. My husband and I aptly nicknamed it "the death diet," because you needed to believe you were dying to stick to it. Finally, I updated my living will with the anticipation that my death was soon to come. I was a shell of myself. I struggled to do even the smallest tasks following a day's work as an assistant property manager. I certainly didn't have the energy or physical ability to continue working nights as a massage therapist, so I let it go.

It was mentally difficult to let go of the massage license and practice I'd worked so hard to obtain. It was also emotionally painful to let go of the clients I'd come to know. But what was particularly challenging for me was accepting that I was sick. I often found myself staring in the mirror or into a doctor's eyes saying, "I'm healthy, goddammit!"

One night in the mystical minutes of the witching hour, a fiery jolt of pain woke me from a dead sleep. As I lay in bed with excruciating throbbing that can be likened only to a broken bone, I contemplated my options and decided I had to get up and do something. I hobbled to the bathroom in search of the doctor-prescribed heavy-dose ibuprofen, and after washing it down with water, I crawled back into bed. Lying there, I prayed the pain would subside so I could fall back to sleep.

As if by some miracle, I not only fell asleep; I also woke up the next morning with an actual spring in my step. I felt great! Like the kind of wonderful that one feels in their early teens or twenties. It was incredible. I made my way to the bathroom to brush my teeth and prepare for the day, feeling overjoyed by this 180-degree turn. Turning the water on and reaching for my toothbrush, I went to toss the prescription bottle in the medicine drawer and noticed it was green. *Oh shit. I took the dog's meds!* I immediately thought.

Our sweet little Mookie, a rescue chihuahua-dachshund mix and twelve pounds of midnight-colored fur, had suffered from multiple health issues his whole life. We regularly gave him prednisone, a steroid, for his asthma. That prescription came in a green bottle, while my meds came in an amber-colored bottle.

Well, it didn't kill me, I thought as I dialed the doctor's office. When the nurse picked up, I had a sense of hope I'd forgotten existed. I finally felt normal! And I couldn't wait to share this accidental discovery that might change everything for me.

Unfortunately, during my appointment, the doctor didn't hear that optimism or excitement, and proceeded to condescend to me once more. He explained that prednisone is a steroid, so of course I felt better; anyone would with a little dose of that. Still, he said it wasn't necessary for what I was dealing with.

After that night, I did my best to move on with all the other paths I was walking along searching for answers and relief. And I continued like this until one morning when I woke up with a reaction that was mirroring anaphylactic shock. Before then, I'd had two anaphylactic reactions in my life, and the symptoms, though mild this time, scared the hell out of me. I immediately called the local clinic to see a doctor. *"Any doctor!"* I screeched through my closing throat at the poor scheduler on the other end of the phone. And that was when the course of my life would change for the decade to come.

That morning, a female doctor walked into the room where I lay on the paper-sheeted exam table. She would become an angel to me, though I doubt she would appreciate my calling her that. With no sense of humor and little patience for small talk, she asked several questions and removed any need for the rushed answers I had become so accustomed to giving. She ordered tests, and when the results came in, she referred me to a rheumatologist. I was poked and prodded throughout all of this, and blood samples upon blood samples were taken. But to start, the rheumatologist put me on a heavy dose of prednisone for pain management.

I knew it!

At the very first visit with the rheumatologist, we discussed my experience and the symptoms' progression. She did not scoff at my theory about the energy exchange with my client. She listened with open ears and an open heart, then encouraged me to keep working backward from there. Like a seasoned improv actor, she responded to the information I shared with "yes and."

"*Yes*, you likely did exchange energy and stirred something up for yourself—*and* there's likely more to the story too," she said. "What happened before that?"

That simple but intelligent question gave my brain the permission it needed to recall the details. I remembered my previous dance classes and how much I missed that creative outlet. Then I remembered why I stopped going. A year before this doctor's appointment I had injured my knee in a dance class and needed surgery. Unfortunately, I'd had an allergic reaction to the anesthesia and as a result, I'd spent the first night following surgery vomiting uncontrollably. That set back my healing time, triggered an autoimmune response in my body, and ultimately ended my ability to dance.

Sitting on the exam table, I realized now that my body was exhausted, that it was revolting and shutting down, and that the symptoms had actually first appeared about a month after that reaction to the anesthesia.

Some people are predisposed to autoimmune diseases, and I happen to be one of them. But working as a massage therapist also had taught me that people often push themselves to the brink of exhaustion or beyond, and their bodies pay the price. I was no different. I had pushed my body during a dance lesson and injured my knee. Following surgery, I had ignored its calls for rest and pushed to continue working as both a property manager and a massage therapist. I had created a breeding ground for illness by ignoring and avoiding my body's needs. You'd think a massage therapist who sprinkled self-care ideas on others like glitter would have picked up on this sooner. But I didn't.

Over time and with the help of incredible doctors, I learned that I was inflamed from the inside out. First the diagnosis was Still's disease, then it was adult-onset juvenile rheumatoid arthritis, then it was full-blown rheumatoid arthritis (RA). Each diagnosis brought heavy drugs with it, which had many side effects. My energy waned, my hair thinned, cramps curled my feet and hands into claws, and I had difficulty breathing at times. All of it was excruciating, both physically and emotionally, but I was still one of the lucky ones. I was blessed with a partner who, although at times struggled with feeling helpless, showed up through thick and thin. With his help, I did my best to remember who I was even when the person reflected in the mirror looked and acted like a stranger.

After years of less expensive drugs failing to work, a doctor offered me the chance to live a normal thirtysomething life again by injecting a tumor necrosis factor (TNF) blocker, a type of medicine that affects the immune system. For those with overactive immune systems, this can be a game-changer. That said, these drugs have serious side effects and require diligence on the patient's part as well as close oversight by a doctor. The road of insurance hurdles to get to this point had been long, and I wasn't about to squander the opportunity, so I said yes to science. I didn't even think twice about overlooking one big possible side effect: cancer. What was this life if I couldn't live it to its fullest? For years, I injected the medication myself and oftentimes combined it with heavy doses of painkillers. By and large, it worked, and I was able to get back to something that resembled normal. I was beyond grateful.

TNF blocker drugs inhibit the immune system. Basically, they make it hard for the body to fight off infections, and as such, there are a few rules to follow. One of the big rules is that if you become ill or have a cut that is an inch or larger, you have to stop taking the drugs so that your body can heal. I managed that pretty well over the years that I took "the good drugs," as I liked to call them. But then twelve years after it all started, I began to experience illnesses that just wouldn't go away. For weeks I yo-yoed from strep throat to yeast infection and back again. It was awful. Finally, on the advice of my rheumatologist, I decided to stop taking the immune-system-blocking drugs for a while. It ended up being the best stroke of luck I'd had in over a decade.

Once I halted the weekly shots of drugs, I put myself back on the death diet. I had hope that it might help heal my ailing gut. I was determined and willing to try anything to stop the horribly uncomfortable swings between strep throat and yeast infection. I cut everything potentially harmful out of my diet, which made enjoying meals rather difficult, but I had a mission: get well, so I could inject the medicine again before the pain returned.

Then something strange happened again.

My RA symptoms didn't return. I wasn't on meds, but I was eating clean. My gut was mostly healed, and I didn't have pain. For three months, I was med-free and pain-free at the same time. What had changed? Why hadn't the diet worked before?

I was in remission. Plain and simple, the inflammation was finally under control and my disease had gone dormant. Sure, I had intermittent flare-ups, but none were as painful as what I'd first experienced. I figured out that if I ate gluten or overdosed on sugar, a flare-up was sure to come. With this knowledge, the need for the full death diet was gone, and I could manage the pain simply by being a bit mindful of what I ate. So, with much deliberation and doctor input, I chose not to return to the heavy-duty drugs I'd taken for so long. I was grateful again, but this time for different reasons.

During that decade of discovery, I learned a lot about who I am and what I'm capable of enduring when put to the test. My patience was tested, my pain tolerance was cracked open and then sealed again, and my core happiness was held together by occasional pain-free, peaceful moments and my husband's love. I learned that nobody is in control to begin with. Something beyond my power threw tar at my feet and slowed down my stride. My life didn't stop; it just moved at a glacial pace. But because of the illness, I started listening to my body as it told me when to push forward and when to rest.

Your Turn

How often do you push yourself to the brink of exhaustion or beyond? And how often do you consider the consequences of doing so? I realize that in the fast-paced world we live in, listening to the body's needs seems like a luxury afforded only to the rich or retired, but I challenge you to think differently. You have every right to hear your body speak to you with its infinite wisdom, and you have the power to listen. I encourage you to tap inward and pay attention to its pleas for rest or its motivation to move.

It is time to slow down and embrace the stillness. You could push through, but now is not the time. Invite rest and welcome the knowledge it brings. Allow your body, mind, and spirit the space they need to reconnect.

Are you listening to them? Can you hold still long enough to listen and hear what they need?

Listen. Rest. Be.

Wife
CHAPTER NINE

I was standing over a sandbox with a handful of small figurines that I'd intuitively picked up only moments before. My job was to place certain ones into the sand however *felt* right. No thinking, no judgment, no logic.

All I felt was discomfort, like a fish out of water. The unease of not knowing what I was doing or why was almost unbearable. I just stood there staring at the sand wondering, *How the hell am I supposed to know what to do with these random figurines in my hands?* Perplexed and a bit frustrated, I tried to remember why I was there: to be open to whatever came; to try something different, since nothing else was working; to discover clarity in my life; and to re-engage my intuition muscle. I closed my eyes and held the eight that I'd chosen. Why any of them had called to me in the first place was beyond logic, but there they were in my hands: three plastic trees, a squirrel, a wolf (or was it a dog or coyote?), an all-black Eskimo carrying a heavy pack, a piece of driftwood, and Isis, the ancient Egyptian Goddess.

From those eight, I chose five. I placed the trees in the sand and then instinctively placed the squirrel beneath their canopy.

I felt my fingers dance in the sand as I drew the small ripples of a stream into its sugary grains beneath the trees. And then the wolf needed to be placed at the stream's opposite end, looking back towards the safe little squirrel.

I took a step back from the scene I'd just intuitively put together. Instantly, I knew what it meant. In my mind, I could stand above it and see that the squirrel was me, safe under the blanket of the trees. Safe under the protection of my husband, who had worked so hard to care for me. But the undercurrent of my life's flow was still beneath me; and at the end of that flowing stream stood the wolf, my intuition, beckoning me to follow her—even if it felt scary.

* * *

By July 2022, when I had this sandbox epiphany in the magic of Sedona, I'd been with my husband, Mike, for twenty-five years. We found each other in 1997, when I was twenty-three years old, and in a sense, we grew up together. When we met, I had a big heart and even bigger dreams. I was born with a creative mind, but even with more than two decades of life under my belt, I still lacked structure in most areas until I met him. In the five years between ages eighteen and twenty-three, I had already lived so many lives. I was the queen of packing up and going, hopping into my car and leaving any situation that didn't suit my needs at any given moment. In fact, I had a rule back then: If it didn't fit in my car, I didn't own it. I had all but perfected fleeing when shit got real or uncomfortable, and then

I met this outspoken, witty, opinionated, funny, kind, giving, charismatic, handsome, and sometimes shy Italian man from Chicago. And everything started to change.

When we met, I was working as a receptionist for an insurance company. He was a college student and part-time swim coach for a country club in Austin, Texas. The owner of the company I was working for was a member of that country club. And, as luck would have it, he was an amateur photographer who had been taking annual pictures of the club's young swim team athletes ever since his children had attended summer camp there. When he asked if I wanted to help with picture day at the club, I immediately responded with a resounding yes. Anything to get out of that office for a day was fine by me.

My job as a helper was to wrangle the children and try to make them look less like wet rats and more like the adorable little freckled munchkins that they were. My future husband's role was to coach them while also handing off the occasional kid to me. Being that he was shy, a simple hello was all he could muster when speaking to me. And since I was convinced I was done with men, like *forever*, I noticed him—his lean, muscular, tan body and the tattoo on his back—but kept moving.

Two weeks after picture day, my life had gone back to normal until the head coach called asking for a copy of the pictures in preparation for the club's annual banquet. He also said, "One of my coaches won't shut up about you. Would you be willing to have coffee with him?"

Well, two coaches had been working that day, so I responded with, "That depends. Is it the one with the tattoo?"

He laughed and said, "As a matter of fact, it is. His name is Mike."

And that was it for me. I hadn't been able to stop thinking about the coach with the tattoo since the day at the pool, and while I wouldn't normally have accepted an invitation like this one, something about Mike's shy demeanor had stuck with me. Soon we were on our first date, laughing together at a comedy club and enjoying a meal at Kerbey Lane Cafe, an Austin original. In fact, I unknowingly picked from the plate of the biggest germaphobe I would come to love.

Once our paths had crossed, the Universe seemed to decide that we would be really good for each other—that we would teach each other patience, kindness, humility, forgiveness, and a slew of other life lessons. Thank God we listened.

It took only one evening together, and I was smitten. I didn't have the wherewithal to balance this new overwhelming love I felt, and my everyday life dissipated like fog in sunlight as I disappeared into new love's bubble. Even my friendships became interwoven into our sanctuary, though I spent less time with friends than I had before. I realize now that this was the beginning of where I started to lose a small part of myself without even noticing I was doing it. All I knew was that I wanted everything good in this world to present itself to this man who brought so much joy into my life. And I would do anything to make that happen.

After only one year of dating, we moved in together and we began to learn the hard lessons of compromise and communication. Then, almost four years later, following a few hiccups, some triumphs, and a short break, he proposed in the most thoughtful way.

At the time, I was working as a retail manager, so my schedule was pretty erratic. It was a blessing if I knew my work schedule two weeks in advance, and rarely did I have a weekend off. Unbeknownst to me, he contacted my boss and asked her to secretly give me a long weekend away from the store. I felt so lucky to have three full days off in a row!

At the end of my last shift before the time away, he showed up unexpectedly at the store to pick me up for dinner. I was thrilled! However, as the escalator carried us to the first floor of the mall, he explained that we weren't going to dinner. Instead, he had arranged for our friends to watch our cats; had packed my bag, which was waiting for me in the car; and had planned a trip to San Francisco. If we didn't hurry, we might miss our flight. I was so surprised, but it still never occurred to me that he might have any ulterior motive for this trip.

For a day and a half, we explored the city. It was new to me, but I instantly loved it for its beauty, diversity, and amazing food. Then another surprise was waiting: He'd rented a car to take us through the California wine country. While I love wine, Mike didn't drink at all back then. He's since found a fruity cocktail he can sip on so I don't drink alone, but back then this was a huge gift and, in my mind, a sacrifice for part of a trip that he had completely planned and paid for. We visited multiple wineries that day, tasting—OK, mostly I was tasting— and laughing. One of the sommeliers we met that day looked and sounded so much like Walter Matthau, I'm still convinced it could have been him. Then came the proposal. In an area overlooking the wetlands at Viansa winery in Sonoma, he got down on one knee. And instantly I said yes.

On our wedding day, the tensions and temperature rose to a hundred degrees. It's funny how weddings, despite being joyous events, bring a certain level of stress for everyone who attends them. I can only imagine it's the heightened energy between souls at a crossroads, a major change in how life will proceed from that day forward. Have you ever noticed how the Universe will throw little or big challenges your way when you're traveling toward change or trying something new that will help your soul expand? Have you noticed that a myriad of happenings occur that try to change your mind, make you late, or push you to the brink of exhaustion? Perhaps, rather than it being the Universe trying to slow us down, it's our own anxious energy flowing outward and reflecting back at us. Maybe it's just us manifesting the difficulties we're struggling with in our mind. To change. To grow. To become who we are meant to be.

Our big day was just that: a day of growth and expansion into who we would become. And all the little fires that popped up throughout the day did their damnedest to divert us, but they ultimately failed to prevent us from solidifying the union we'd already created. His tux arrived but was a size too small. We wondered whether my dad would make it on time to walk me down the aisle. The guest book arrived late and subsequently remains empty to this day. During our first dance, the music accidentally got turned off. We were poked, prodded, tripped, and pushed as we took those first steps toward the one commitment that would challenge us more than we could imagine. Looking back on that day, I see a blissfully happy young woman who had a picture in her head about who she should become following her vows. A picture that I didn't necessarily paint on my own.

"Two Become One."

Those words were engraved on a small sign that hung in my dad and stepmom's house. Words that I reflected on often leading up to and immediately following the wedding. The scripture condensed is basically, "Two shall become one flesh." Meaning that two whole people, when married, are to unite as one in every way—emotionally, intellectually, financially, spiritually, and in life purpose. In my mind, that meant that a husband and wife should be so close that they function as if they are one person. They support each other through their strengths and weaknesses. In a more day-to-day, practical manner, I imagined and believed that my role was to care for him. To put his needs first. To become a part of him. These were ideals I held in my head that would lead to a successful marriage, and I was more than willing to embrace them. I just may have over-indexed on them a bit.

Our time together in the first years of marriage brought challenges, happiness, and a lot of change. We bought our first home, where I discovered the joy of nesting, cooking, cleaning, and caring for my husband along with our two cats and three dogs. I started perfecting the art of caretaking. Without ever being asked, I began to embody what I envisioned a picture-perfect wife to be based on the models I'd learned from. And I enjoyed it!

In fact, together we embraced a belief that I still hold true to this day: place commitment for each other over the daily grind and ego-driven wants. This has served us well, and as long as both people in the relationship are willing to buy into it, the method can be effective for individual and collective happiness. Thankfully, we both adopted and continue to hold on to this way of thinking.

Over the years, we shared our stories. And I found myself starting to put his tiny and big hurts before my own. This was the perfect excuse for me to bury the shit from my childhood that I didn't want to face. After all, I'd had a perfect upbringing, right? I was fine and didn't need to face anything uncomfortable. Sweep it all under a cute little rug and focus on what he needed in order to heal. As I saw it, he needed to experience unconditional love and someone who would show up for everything, every time. Baseball games every week? I was there. All-nighters to learn and produce work? I'd do my best to stay up when he let me, which rarely happened. Cook almost every meal every day? Absolutely. I did all these things joyfully and am happy that I got to experience them with him.

These gifts of my time were a way of sharing and showing the love I felt for him. They were beautiful gifts to give, but they came with a price. I unintentionally left little to no time for myself in the process. I failed to notice that in giving all my energy and time to him, I wasn't caring for myself. I wasn't refilling my own tank. I lost my balance. I let go of acting, then dance, meditation, and reading books on the world's mystical curiosities. I let go of my connection to the Universe and buried the mystic creative living in my soul's center. Mike never once asked me to give up on my passions, and I didn't release my grip on them overnight. It happened slowly over time. I didn't really even notice unless someone asked me what my interests or hobbies were. My blank stare offering insight into pieces of me that were missing, I would then make half-hearted attempts to unearth them before distracting myself as a caretaker or by burying myself in work once again.

Over those years, I had many conversations with female friends who had also forgotten what their hobbies had once been. We'd sit for hours over glasses of wine discussing how we didn't understand how our partners or husbands easily knew that they loved baseball, golf, cars, music...the list went on. It was baffling how the men had time to devote to such things. We were left to work ridiculous hours filling the needs of our coworkers and clients, clean up and chase after our children's needs (OK, their kids, not mine), care for aging parents, or simply keep making a house a home. It was all on us to make it happen.

What a load of bullshit.

I kept this way of thinking planted front and center in my head for so many years, I lost count. And I did so with a smile on my face, because I actually loved and took pride in being a caretaker. In being the one others could always count on—especially the one Mike could always count on. Whether it was at the expense of my personal growth was irrelevant. I was there showing up every day for my loved ones and anyone else who would let me. I thought I was doing it right.

Then the pandemic hit. I was working as a director of the management services department for a real estate company. On a normal day there were so many balls in the air, I never would have noticed if dicks had started springing up from the floor like flowers. But when that unprecedented event that brought the world to a halt came flying out of the woodwork, I hit my limit. My tank was already empty, regardless of whether I'd briefly been on a cyclical and half-hearted attempt to refuel. I not only needed a full tank for the journey I was facing at the onset of COVID; I needed a reserve gas can in the trunk. I broke down. Or rather, I decided enough was enough. Although I had committed to leading that team at work, I needed to retreat for the sake of my own health. True to our marital agreement, Mike stepped up and we started planning our next move.

We needed nature, national parks, and seasons. We also needed to escape from hundred-degree heat and mosquitos. So, we set our sights on Colorado, and I set my sights on a step down in my career. *Perhaps less responsibility will create more time for me*, I thought.

This was a phenomenal idea that I didn't execute well. I created more time but still failed to face the truth about my inbred habit of ignoring what my mind, body, and soul were craving. I was still avoiding my interest in mystical curiosities. I was waiting for Mike to join me on hikes rather than venturing out on my own. Due to the pandemic, I wasn't going to improv classes or seeking out other creative outlets. And I was actively finding excuses to not write or paint. I had different scenery and weather, but my tendencies to circumvent self-care continued. As a result, I felt more and more unbalanced.

Then, in the spring of 2021, following quick, uneducated, and scarcity-driven decisions, Mike and I faced a significant challenge when we purchased a lemon house. Through the tumultuous experience, through rotten floors and asbestos-ridden walls, we discovered the undying strength of our true connection. Living in hotels and in the guest room of newly found friends, we would regularly wake up in tears. Finding ways to console each other through the fear that we'd lost our life's savings along with the security that we'd worked so hard to build, we were pulled together once again by the Universe. In twenty years of marriage, we'd faced many obstacles. Thankfully, through communication and caring for each other, we made our way through this one as well.

I couldn't help but notice, however, that the Universe had taken me by the shoulders and was aggressively shaking me. "WAKE UP!" she screamed.

My house was literally falling apart around me. My job was shifting in a way that felt so far from what I thought I had wanted. All of it signaled the need for a significant shift in direction. I didn't know what that direction should be, but I knew I needed to change something. So, with Mike's support, I left my job and a month later went to Sedona for a life-changing soul adventure that started with me playing in the sand. The discoveries were mind-blowing and heart-opening. I felt so free and full of life again. For the first time in a long time, I was excited about what the future held for me. Not for us. Not for him. For me.

On a normal day, that would have felt so selfish to admit or say out loud. But this was no normal day. This was a soul-discovery trip just for me. And somewhere across the 700 miles I drove, during that week I spent without technology (other than a daily check-in with Mike), I restored my childlike wonder. I reopened the internal portal that allows me the ability to see past lives, commune with ancestors, and connect with higher realms. And I rediscovered my intuition's voice. I was renewed. Reborn.

When I got home, I was so full of excitement about the clarity I'd received in Sedona that I word-vomited all of it onto Mike. Without considering the impact it might have on him or our life plan, I cheered, "This is what I want to do!" I explained that I essentially wanted to be a motivational speaker, to help people rediscover their balance in life and introduce them to the holistic view of balance. To help educate people about how balance encompasses our feminine and masculine energy, how it brings about harmony, and how we can achieve it individually and as a collective whole. I decided to take a sharp left turn in life and leave my well-paid profession to start my own business—without a plan. And because I was so excited, he supported me. And has supported me ever since. Amazing, right?

Yes and no. I was still off-balance. Yes, I was excited. Overjoyed. Like a kid in a candy store. But off-balance in my marriage and in my self-regulation.

If I had that moment to do over, I would likely take a step back to have a discussion with Mike about what that change in my career and life direction might look like, and how it might affect our shared trajectory into retirement and our golden years. I might work with him to devise a business plan and head into the new venture with eyes wide open. But often, when we bury ourselves for too long, we come out swinging. For me, I came out dancing and singing. And luckily for me, he was there for it—cheering me on even if it was with a little hesitation or fear for what could happen if I failed.

Since that day, I have worked diligently to continue to listen to my soul's needs. To pay attention to the impulses that my intuition knows to be right and true. But I've also worked to communicate those feelings and nudges with Mike in a way that holds space for our collective needs too. I haven't always done it perfectly, but I've come to accept that learning to balance caring for the man I love more than anything with caring for myself will be a work in progress. Some days I will get it right, and some days I'll just need to chalk it up to a good try. Because in the end (or the middle, where we currently seem to be), I have learned that there's a difference between making your partnership a priority and putting yourself last.

Rediscovering my balance hasn't been easy or pretty. I've fucked it up as many times as I've gotten it right, and there have been times when I've slipped back into old patterns. I suspect that will continue for as long as I live. But the difference now is that I recognize when I'm doing it, I notice that it doesn't feel good, and I make a conscious effort to course-correct. If you were to ask me today what my hobbies are, I wouldn't stare at you blankly. I would say, "Hiking with my dog, and with Mike, if he feels like joining; reading; learning about human connections to one another, to Mother Earth, and to the Universe; painting; watching binge-worthy TV shows; and cooking." It takes daily commitment to consciously choose who comes first and for how long. I have to make a concerted effort to carve out time for my hobbies, to meditate and journal so that I stay grounded, to continue learning about the mystical curiosities of the universe, and to venture out into nature all by my lonesome. I am thankful that I consciously nurture these personal loves and passions, and that I do so while also nurturing and caring for the love of my life. I am grateful to be awake and fully aware of how I choose to live as an individual, and how I choose to show up as Mike's wife.

Your Turn

What would you say if I were to ask you today, "What are your hobbies?" Or what would you do? Would you stare at me blankly, slowly blinking your eyes only to ease the tension of your vacant gaze?

This is your wake-up call. Act now, before the Universe slaps you in the face, begging you to wake from your slumber and embrace all the gifts that you've been given. Make a list of all the things you used to do that made you happy or brought you joy. Before the job, before a marriage or other relationship, before any kids, what did those little loves or passions consist of? How does it feel to just remember what they once were? In the past, what did you enjoy doing or learning about? Fold that list up or close the book where you jotted them down and walk away from it for a day. You've done your part for now.

Then return to it the next day. Don't wait too long. Don't let that feeling go stale. Reopen those feelings and let them tingle their way into your feet. Experience the grounded feeling that comes from acknowledging what you once found interesting. Stare at the list, run your fingertips over it, and then circle the one thing that highlights itself for you. You will know—your heart will know—even if your mind doesn't. Trust that call and don't judge it. Let it present what your soul needs you to spend time with, focus on, and learn about.

Now it's time. It's time to carve out fifteen minutes for yourself each day. If you have more than that some days, wonderful. But your commitment is fifteen minutes—because that is doable no matter what. The one love that lit up when you hovered over your list is calling to you. Will you answer? In fifteen minutes a day, your soul will thank you.

No matter where you are in life, it is OK to seek the truth about who you are. To choose a different path.
To ask questions and find the answers within.

To focus on you.

Those who love you will be by your side as you transform. There is nothing to fear.

Property Manager
CHAPTER TEN

The wave of complaints was cresting, and I was convinced the full moon was to blame. Anytime the moon reached the howling phase, every office manager, human resources director, and admin assistant who rented office space self-proclaimed their position to be assistant property manager and came out in droves to make sure I was aware that something was bothering them that day. And until that moon transitioned to the next phase, they would do this daily until every nit had been picked sufficiently.

Scanning the parking lot from my circa-1990s mahogany desk—it was now 2014—I was thankful that our office was on the ground floor, with windows that faced the building opposite where I sat. I'd worked in corporate offices, makeshift offices, and even once in a closet, so I was thrilled to take this job managing two high-end office buildings in the Austin suburbs and to discover that my office was expected to mirror the class A atmosphere of the properties. Sure, the property owner expected our team to sprint outside whenever a work truck attempted to park in front of either building and redirect the driver to a special parking space in the garage, but I had windows! This privilege was never lost on me.

I'd landed this job when an acquaintance who would later become a friend recommended me. She loved it, and the role of senior property manager overseeing two four-story buildings was a step up from the lesser role I'd held for over four years managing nine class B office, retail, and industrial buildings. I'd been ready for a change, and after one year, I was for the most part incredibly happy I'd taken the leap. The property management company was supportive of its employees, and our boss was tough but fair. Looking at the big picture, I had it pretty good. But day after day, the grinding stress of managing people's complaints started weighing on me. I clung to my happy-go-lucky demeanor with the tight grip of my unpolished nails, and yet I just couldn't shake the negative feelings that were bubbling up beyond my control. Even on a day when the only clouds in the bluest sky were dotted cords of billowy fluff, I couldn't control the rage that was welling up inside.

On this otherwise beautiful day, having just hung up the phone after talking with the longest-standing tenant in the building, the overwhelming urge to hit something (or someone) bubbled up. The words of their office manager, Brianna, echoed in my head.

"Did you hear what I said? I placed that paper clip under the conference room table over a week ago, and it's still there! I'm telling you the night crew is not doing their job. They aren't even vacuuming! What are you going to do about it?"

Well-rehearsed placating words fell from my lips despite what I really wanted to say, "I understand why this could be upsetting. I'll talk with the supervisor and get this taken care of right away. Is there anything more I can help with?"

I leaned forward in defeat, cupping my forehead with my hand. A guttural sigh came from somewhere deep within me.

Losing count of the complaints about the janitorial crew that had come in over the past two days and knowing I couldn't fix them all immediately, I opened up some financial reports that I was expected to complete by day's end. I hoped to create some quiet time and focus my attention on them. I had learned long before that my strength came from allowing myself time to slow down and catch mistakes before I put my stamp of approval on any report. Unfortunately, just as I was fastening the "math hat" atop my head, the phone rang again—and this time the caller had a legitimate complaint.

A construction crew in the building next door had set up a workstation outside the building's main entrance. Clients were walking into the building through sparks being thrown from saws cutting metal pipes. Brent, our chief building engineer, overheard the discussion and called, "I'm on it" over his shoulder as he headed out the door. But since this was the fifth time I'd had the same conversation with this contractor, I grabbed my hard hat and jogged to catch up to him.

Entering the building, we politely asked the workers to stop cutting pipes, and proceeded to the vacant space where we knew the superintendent would be. It was in complete disarray as it awaited a transformation, so I carefully positioned my heels between cords and weaved around men on ladders running cable above the ceiling tiles. I got a whiff of burning wires as jackhammering assaulted my ears. The noise was so loud that the walls shook. I could feel my blood starting to boil as I reread texts from my company's assistant manager, alerting us to the many complaints coming in about this noise specifically.

Brent pulled back a dingy clear piece of plastic hanging from the open ceiling grid, revealing a temporary staging area that housed project plans, stale coffee, and a makeshift meeting area. Sitting there staring back at us blankly, feet propped up on a fold-out table that doubled as a desk, was the superintendent himself.

His complete disregard for the noise and the fact that his subs were creating absolute havoc made me exasperated. The words vomited from my mouth at a speed my Texas drawl didn't recognize as I berated him and questioned his work ethic. "What in the hell do you think you're doing? There is absolute chaos happening around you! Do you just not give a shit? Get off your ass and control your subs. You get paid to be an asshole, not me. So do your job!"

Never having been that aggressive in my work interactions before, I left before I could start crying.

Somewhere between this, the myriad of complaints, and those looming financial reports, I began to lose sight of the kindness I usually so intentionally tried to lead with. Back at my desk, I caught myself mindlessly toggling between computer screens. I was so dysregulated that I couldn't even prioritize simple work. I knew I had to get my shit together, so I hit the pause button on my workday and walked outside.

Fortunately, behind the building there was a crushed-granite trail surrounded by oak trees that meandered in the most unassuming way, allowing its wanderers to disappear for a short while. When I stepped onto the trail, I practiced a quick meditation I'd done a million times, one that I could do while walking.

> **Birds. Traffic. Wind**, I silently intoned, to focus on all the stuff swirling around me.
>
> **The breeze feels cool. The sun feels warm.** To focus on the sensation on my skin.
>
> **Breathe in the air I feel. Breathe out.** To focus inward.
>
> **Left. Right. Left. Right.** To focus on the souls of my feet as they touched the ground.

And just like that, my cup was refilled a little more than halfway, and it was time to get on with the day ahead.

As I reentered the office, I could hear the phone ringing. I was hoping it wasn't another construction complaint, but with my newly regulated nervous system, I was prepared for whatever might come. I planted the biggest toothy grin I could muster on my face so that cheerfulness could naturally flow through my voice, and picked up the phone.

It wasn't at all what I'd expected. On the other end of the line was Katherine, the main contact for one of our larger tenants in the building and one of the nicest humans I had ever met. She was clearly in a state of shock. In a hushed tone, she asked if I could please come to their suite as quietly and quickly as possible. They had just received an active-shooter threat.

I discreetly made my way to their suite with Brent by my side. I kept thinking that surely there'd been a mistake. We were in the suburbs, and stuff like this didn't happen in our neck of the woods.

Boy, was I wrong.

As we stood in this rather large company's lobby, I felt the inconsequential stress of the morning fade. None of it mattered anymore as I looked into the eyes of the receptionist, who had just taken the call. The police had been summoned and were asking her questions as she tried to recall what happened. She seemed like she was trying to recapture memories that were disappearing like smoke. I imagine it was hard for her to recall details because her brain was focused on protecting her from the traumatic threat.

The police officers peppered her with questions. "Was it a man or a woman? Did they have an accent? What kind of accent? What exactly did they say? Were there any noises in the background—people talking, traffic, or office noise? Do you remember the number that came through on caller ID? Can you scroll through the phone and find it now?"

She was clearly in shock, scared, and shutting down. One of the police officers, giving the receptionist a moment to collect herself, turned to Brent and me. He called us over to the side and questioned us about the building. We answered dutifully and asked about making an announcement to all the tenants. He directed us to wait while he and his partner determined if this was a real threat.

I once again inquired about measures to protect the people in the building. To my surprise, he responded that it wasn't his concern at that moment. This caught me completely off guard. Then I startled myself and Brent when, in a moment of frustration, I snapped and emphasized the gravity of our responsibility for everyone's safety in the building. I had never once talked back to a police officer before, and it felt out of character. The officer's patient eyes met mine and I calmed my tone, telling him I understood—even though I didn't. The officer assured me that the car they'd parked at the front entrance to the building would remain in place, and then went back to questioning the receptionist.

Brent and I returned to our office as instructed and tried to act normally. The police didn't seem overly concerned. Only one squad car was onsite, and most people didn't even notice it. Just as I was beginning to think I had overreacted, the phone rang again. The company had received a second threat.

After leaving their suite for the second time, we now had a new directive. We were to lock the entrances to the buildings; people could leave but not enter. Our job was to send out an email to alert only the main contacts for each company. Inform but don't incite panic.

We called the asset manager for our building and the property management director. Then I sent out a carefully crafted email with the "run, hide, fight" information that was usually distributed only during annual fire drills. A few questions came back quickly, but those who did reach out were patient with us and our limited amount of information.

An hour passed, but my nerves were still on high alert, and any movement in the parking lot immediately caught my peripheral attention. I was starting to feel like we were in the clear. The police were still present, but only two remained, which seemed promising. If they didn't think the situation was earth-shattering, then I shouldn't either.

It was eerily quiet in our office. You could hear the clicking of keyboards and the occasional throat clearing. The tension was palpable. When the phone rang once more, everything stopped. For a split second, we all looked at each other with the unspoken hope that this would be good news.

It wasn't.

A third call had come through, and this time it had been a bomb threat with very specific information about our building. Thankfully, the receptionist who'd been rattled earlier had pulled herself together and was a quick study. With the help of the police, she'd been able to get a lot more information out of the caller. And just like that, the threat escalated to something much more real. We were instructed to have our building and the one next door to us evacuated immediately.

We sent emails and made calls to our day porters, contractors, and any vendors working at the building. Considering the authorities' instruction to use extreme caution so we didn't cause panic, and all property managers' CYA (cover your ass) approach, I also emailed the tenants about needing to evacuate quietly. Getting something in writing was always the first rule of thumb for any important correspondence. But as soon as I hit Send, I second-guessed my decision and thought, *That isn't good enough.* This was not the time to assume people read their emails. And so, feeling like easy targets, the assistant and I called the tenants one by one, alerting them to the situation as calmly as possible. We weren't prepared for an event like this. Up to this point, we had needed only a simple call sheet to reference occasionally when picking up the phone to make a call or two. We had never needed to call every single tenant in a matter of minutes. I felt like a sitting duck. Meanwhile, the building engineers were ushering people out of each building and trying to keep everyone calm as they evacuated. Once we had called everyone we could, I asked the assistant to help with crowd control outside while I assisted the engineers with evacuating the final few people.

It was surreal to be standing my ground at the building's entrance while floods of people exited, wondering if there was a bomb somewhere ticking down to its last second. Index finger to lips, I quietly encouraged people to stay calm and off social media.

As soon as it seemed the buildings were empty, I stepped outside and met the police in the middle of the parking lot. Several police cars had arrived, but there was no bomb squad to be seen.

Then things got really weird.

Brent and I met with the officer in charge. With wide eyes and a naivety I'll never regain, I asked what their plan was. My main concern was how soon we could re-enter after they'd swept the building for the bomb. Any property manager worth her weight in gold knows that the duty to the financial safety of the landlord is of the utmost importance, and the last thing anyone would want was a slew of tenants demanding rent relief for forced closures and lost revenue. I was dumbfounded when the officer informed us that they wouldn't sweep the property. From their perspective, no one had actually seen a bomb—there was only the threat of one.

As if that weren't enough to throw anyone into a tailspin, they proceeded to advise us that Brent and I would be the ones to have to sweep the building for the bomb. From their point of view, they knew less than we did about what was or wasn't out of place at the building. We were, in their minds, better equipped for the job.

When I get into a confrontation, my mind often goes blank. I'm one of those people who search the mind's corners for the right words only to find that those words are experts at hiding when stress is involved. And in this moment, I was speechless—until the fear caught up and the words poured out. "Are you fucking kidding me?!"

Brent took a step forward and addressed the officer kindly. I stepped to the side and called Sarah, our director of property management, to bring her up to speed. I informed her of the situation and let her know that we wouldn't be able to reopen the building until it could be swept and considered safe, but that there was no way I was asking anyone on the team to do that work—myself included. She immediately said that there was no way she would have allowed that anyway.

Instead, she started calling around to find a private company with a bomb-sniffing dog. We quickly learned that there were only two bomb-sniffing dogs in the state of Texas for hire, and neither was available to work at our building. The next thing I knew, I got a call about a California-based firm that specialized in threats just like the one we were facing. They were sending out a team to make sure we were all safe, and they would be there the next day.

My immediate orders? Keep the buildings locked up. Send people home. And again, stay off social media.

The weekend that followed brought a prolonged cold sweat, the kind that appears when your body doesn't know what to do with the stress it's experiencing. I met the team of four at the property the next morning and waited nervously while they searched the buildings high and low. And finally, they appeared empty-handed. Relief swept over me.

Over the next few months, training, learning, planning, and preparing for the worst to occur again would engulf me. In the beginning, it would feel like drinking water from a fire hydrant as I soaked up all the information I could.

What were the accessible high points in the building where shooters could position themselves? Where were the exposed areas below, and how could I get people to safety while diverting those areas? What were our refuge areas, and how should I train hundreds of people to evacuate to them safely? How could I keep people from evacuating to the parking garages, given that bomb threats most often are made to lure people precisely to that area?

Things I never knew existed, let alone thought I would have to learn about, were suddenly being thrown at me. It quickly became clear that we had to devise a better system for the future. So I got to work.

Eliminating as many threats to our internal team as I could, we changed the emergency notification protocol. Never again would we call tenants one by one. Instead, we enlisted a third party's help to create pre-recorded messages that could be auto-dialed and auto-texted.

We also changed our view of what to expect from emergency personnel. No longer would we depend on law enforcement to guide us while sitting ignorantly on the sidelines blindly taking orders. We held meetings with tenants and incorporated refuge areas into fire drills. We drew up more robust evacuation plans and created protocols for extreme emergencies.

Was I ever going to be fully trained for another event like this? Hell no. But I wasn't going to be a sitting duck anymore either.

Once the dust settled, life went back to normal. Complaints and calls continued to pour in, and construction-induced disruptions resumed. However, at least to the team that led evacuations and pulled together through uncertainty, none of these daily events or occurrences ever felt like more than a small inconvenience.

Your Turn

In one day, I experienced the full range of stress that can occur at any point when working as a property manager. It isn't uncommon to feel different types of stress on any given day, but to encounter all within a matter of hours is an anomaly. And while I'd already realized the importance of resilience and bravery, on this day I was reminded of the impact that perspective can have on our ability to maintain balance and manage any kind of situation.

The next time you find yourself feeling all the feels that come from stress, change your breathing pattern, your scenery or surroundings, or maybe even your shoes. Shift something physical to create awareness of your mental and emotional state. This can help you become grounded—present. And once you have regulated your nervous system, you'll be able to access the parts of your brain that control vocabulary and reasoning. You'll also find yourself much more open to different perspectives.

Shift your perspective and shift the energy back in your favor.

This is not happening to you; it's happening for you. It's here to teach you something, so accept things as they are in this moment, for nothing ever stays the same. You will learn and grow from this.

Trust that what you're facing right now will evolve, and that you will evolve with it. Trust that you've been given this challenge for a reason, and that you are right where you're supposed to be.

Friend
CHAPTER ELEVEN

When Christa and I were friends, we were in our early twenties and in need of love wherever we could find it. She was the epitome of fun. Her laugh would ring through a room, and she could make any situation more enjoyable. Welcoming her as a sister, my family and I invited her in as if she were one of our own. She joined mother-daughter trips I took with my mom and sister, was by my side at family dinners and other get-togethers, and was included in every gathering with friends—even with the friends I'd known since grade school.

We met through mutual acquaintances on a night out at a dance club in Denver, where the music was so loud I could feel the bass pulse in my chest. When a man asked me to the dance floor, instead of saying yes, I offered up the hand of this young woman I'd met only moments before. Was it just to see what she might do? Or was it to test the waters of whether we could be friends? Whatever the motivation, it worked. We became friends instantly, and best friends in a remarkably short amount of time.

While living in Denver in the mid-nineties, we became roommates, but also so much more. We shared moments of greatness and sadness. I told her my secrets, and she told me hers. But six months into our friendship we would end up living in different states—she would go on an adventure following a boy, and I would go back home to Texas, needing time with my mom following a monumental shift in our family dynamic.

In 1996, my grandma passed away after a long battle with lung cancer. I remember a cartoon drawing she had hung on her wall when she was going through chemo: it was of a pelican holding a frog in its beak, trying to enjoy the meal, but the frog was hanging in there—its front legs were stretched out, and its feet were grasping the pelican by its throat. At the bottom of the poster, it read, "Never Give Up." My grandma was a spitfire and the matriarch in my life, and when she passed away, my life became a mess. Searching to fill the void, I would flounder and fill it with what I could. However, with Christa no longer by my side to help me walk through the storm, I felt lost. She was hours away by car, and I thought she was happy. I didn't want to burden her with my sadness or my mistakes that were piling up.

But then, she called. She'd had a heart-wrenching breakup, and she wanted me to pick her up and bring her to Texas.

So I drove to New Orleans, Louisiana and got her. We nursed each other back to being the carefree girls we once had been, spending our days in South Austin swimming at our apartment community's pool, giggling, and pretending we had money to shop at the stores we browsed endlessly.

Soon after, we both met and fell in love with men almost at the exact same time. It was as if kismet had decided for the four of us to come together. We laughed, shared meals, and felt connected almost on a soul level. We went everywhere together, sharing our lives, and I thought we would be a chosen family for the rest of our days.

Christa was there for all of the big and small moments, including the ups and downs, tasks, and events that go with planning a wedding. Although I wanted my mom by my side as I picked out my dress, that wasn't in the cards for me. I can't remember why she couldn't be there; I just remember feeling her absence as I shopped and tried on dress after dress. Christa, however, was all-in and even found *the* dress for me. There, on a mannequin in the middle of the David's Bridal Shop, stood a princess-like gown that I adored and that, low and behold, was on sale for a hundred and fifty dollars. Since my fiancé and I had chosen to pay what we could for the wedding, knowing our parents didn't have the means to help, this find was huge for our budget. Besides, I felt like a million bucks in it.

On the big day, as I shared vows with the man I wanted to spend my life with, she stood right there by my side.

When the first few years of marriage were challenging, as my new husband and I learned to communicate, compromise, and find our rhythm, she was my sounding board, offering perspective and levity. And I played that role for her. We found safety in confiding in and providing support for each other. We shared the sorrow when we lost fur babies who had grown old.

She was there as my dream of being an actress started to erode, and she was there when I got sick. I trusted that she would always be there, because she was a constant in my life.

Years later, at her request, I got ordained as a minister online and officiated at her wedding. As she and the man she loved shared vows, I held back tears of happiness as I witnessed their moment. And my husband took the pictures that captured the story of their day. We were still together, the four of us.

In a way, we were growing up together. We both bought our first homes in Texas only about fifteen minutes from each other. We went on vacations together, and Christa's new husband even coined the term "bacation"—a nod to how we would overdose on bacon while away. Christa and I even tried to start a business selling handmade journals. It didn't go very far, but I think the whole reason we did it to begin with was to make sure we spent time together as our adult lives were taking shape. We were always looking for ways to stay connected. We even sent in a videotaped audition for *The Amazing Race*—yes, that was before the invention of the smartphone.

Then life got hard, as Christa started moving through her own difficulties. Her dad passed away, and I wasn't there as I should have been. Instead of showing up at her house and holding her, I asked her to call me anytime—day or night. It was then that I learned the lesson about grief and supporting those we love who are going through it the hard way. It's easy to say, "What do you need?" or, "How can I help?" or, "Call me anytime, day or night." But if you really want to show up for the person who needs you, you have to be willing to do the hard thing. Just show up—on their doorstep—and sit with them. Hold them while they cry and maybe cry a little too. Sit in it with them, agree that it sucks, and show them through your actions that they are not alone.

From that point forward, our relationship was strained. When we would meet up, she wanted to vent about the frustrations of marriage or work, and I became hardened to her words. All I could hear was complaints and negativity. No longer could I feel the empathy she so needed me to have with her. It felt like if I didn't reciprocate with a dump truck full of complaints, then I wasn't someone she could trust. I felt fake— searching for things to bitch about so she wouldn't feel alone in her frustrations. I didn't know how to navigate the new rules of our relationship, and instead of talking about it, I slowly pulled away. Little by little, I moved further from her heart, and she could sense it.

We no longer spent our time together giggling or sharing the light, but rather searching for a way to share what was wrong. It was heavy, and I wanted to set the weight down for a while. I didn't want to walk away forever; I wanted space to embrace positivity and to no longer feel like I was the plate that all of the leftover negative helpings got scraped onto as the table was cleared.

It was ugly and unscripted when I asked for that space. I was cruel in pulling back the energy that I'd so freely given for so many years. When I did, she fought back. And I didn't fight at all. At the time, I thought it was kind to stop myself from saying things I couldn't take back. She threw punches so hard, it left scars on my relationships with the people around us. We were so intertwined, there was likely no way we would have been able to separate without some scars, but at the time I felt so betrayed.

Then she was gone. Forever.

Those scars would harden my willingness to let others in for years to come. My ability to trust and create friendships was stunted. Rather than show the real me or share my ups and downs with others, I would become hidden and quiet. No one would know what was truly going on with me by looking at my surface, but I did. I knew I would never let another friend beyond the superficial levels of my skin. Never again would I share the intricacies of my feelings or thoughts. Never again would I be open to allowing a friend to truly know me.

Never say *never*.

In the years that followed, I had dreams about her. My heart and soul missed her so deeply, we would visit while I slept, talking and giggling as we had done so many times before...all those times when I'd taken her presence for granted. I thought about calling, but each time the idea rang in my thoughts, I would remember the negativity, the hurtful words, and the toll that our relationship and our separation had taken on my life. So I would hang up the metaphorical phone and move on with my day. But often I wondered what life would have been like if we'd stayed friends. I missed the closeness that can occur only between women.

Then I met two older, wiser, and patient souls. I met each of them separately through our work as property managers. I would see them at industry events, or we'd work together periodically for the same company. They would come and go from my life over several years. It wasn't until we attended the funeral of a mutual acquaintance who had died unexpectedly from a heart attack in her thirties that we started intentionally scheduling time to meet up as friends.

Although I'm as different from each of them as three people can be, strangers often ask if we're sisters. Emma is just slightly shorter than I am, and if she's standing straight, she'll tell you she's five foot five. She has greenish blue eyes, olive skin, and dark blonde hair that often falls just below her shoulders. She's a runner, a painter, a reader, and the best teller of dad jokes I've ever heard. Jess is a tall drink of water, towering over me and Emma. Once a professional ballerina, she has a strong body that carries her with grace into any room, and as we've discovered while shopping for ridiculous outfits or prom dresses, she somehow looks fabulous in everything. She makes us laugh when we least expect it, and has the wit and wisdom of someone twice her age.

We weren't instant friends—I was still so guarded. But they invited me in, and without expectation of reciprocation, they shared their thoughts and feelings. They shared their lives. Slowly and with the gentleness of crones, of wise women, they peeled away my layers of distrust and hurt. They brought out the hidden person who so wanted to love friends like sisters once again. However, this time, they taught me how to love and hold space for the dark days they were going through without feeling the full weight of it all.

As I opened up my true self to them, the beauty of sisterhood once again invited me in. We spent countless hours dancing in the kitchen, sharing wine, and exploring all that the Texas hill country had to offer. Then I moved to Colorado in 2020 and Jess moved to Massachusetts in 2021. When these big transitions were happening for us, we were all a little afraid that we might lose touch. We were afraid that this "Golden Girls coven" we'd carefully created would begin to fragment and fall apart. But it didn't! With intention and effort, we managed to maintain our connection. Each year planning out trips to get together, we filled the time in between with phone calls and video chats. I dare say that although we are physically miles apart, our hearts are closer than we could have ever imagined.

At the expense of one of my closest relationships in this life, I learned that empathy without absorption is possible, especially when we're willing to speak from a calm and understanding space. And with the chisels of new friends, patient enough to find a few cracks where light could be let in, I also learned that authentic connections come when you share your whole self—blemishes and all.

Your Turn

Have you been burned and thought, *That's it, I'm never trusting anyone with my heart again*? Being vulnerable with someone—opening up your true self to expose the most fragile parts—is terrifying enough on its own. But if you've built walls around your heart brick by brick after someone has unexpectedly turned your soft middle inside out, it takes real bravery to dismantle them. I know how scary it is to take a sledgehammer to those walls, but the alternative leads to a lonely existence and one where you miss out on one of the most beautiful parts of life—connection. People come into our lives when it's time for us to learn from each other, or perhaps as part of a soul-family connection. People go from our lives when we've both learned what we can from one another, or when we allow ourselves to release ancestral attachments and wounds. Whether you handle the departure of a person from your life with or without grace, cut yourself some slack and learn from the experience. Forgive yourself, forgive the other person, and open up your heart to learn from someone new.

Find a quiet spot, close your eyes, breathe, and imagine swinging a hammer as you break down the walls around your heart. Can you be brave and invite new souls into your life?

You will love again. Your heart will heal, and you'll learn to trust once more.

For now, be patient. Be kind to yourself and remember who you are—who you came here to be. Then open your energy. Let it spill out onto the streets and ripple into the hearts of others. For soon you will connect with new souls who will ride with you on the roller coaster of life and who will love you just for who you are.

Executive
CHAPTER TWELVE

After working as a property manager for over a decade, I landed a role as a director in the real estate industry. While I was often the only woman in the room or one of two women seated at the conference table, I felt confident that I'd earned my spot. No one had given it to me. In the early days of my newly found leadership position, I kept notes and reminders in a notebook that my husband had gifted me in celebration of my new position. The cover read, "Good Things Come to Those Who Work Their Asses Off." That was my mantra, and it had served me well. With no college degree, no special schooling, and no leg up through family ties, I had worked my way up into a true leadership role. I finally had a seat at the table, but I can't say I was one hundred percent prepared to be there.

While I was a whiz at operations, I had a lot to learn when it came to business development and managing the weight of being responsible for the success of a company and its employees. I knew how to run teams and be a mentor; however, the artful balance between being the company's liaison and the people's leader was something entirely different. There was so much fun to be had, but there were also a lot of sleepless nights—an entirely new territory I found myself trying to traverse.

Self-care was the first thing to go. No longer having the energy to exercise, I rarely went to the gym. Instead, I committed full force to reconstructing the processes, client relations, and team operations at the company. And I loved every second of it, so I didn't allow myself to notice when I felt tired, gained weight, or lost time with loved ones. After all, it wasn't supposed to be easy.

Not recognizing that quiet time is productive, I began each workday cramming in team calls from my car on the way to the office. Drawing from my experience as an onsite property manager, I was particularly sensitive to the potential feelings of isolation that could arise among team members. Since the majority of our teams were dispersed across towns and states, I started creating connection opportunities for everyone the moment I stepped into a leadership role. My favorite moments were those that allowed me to craft experiences and a feeling of community within our groups—the kind of experiences that made it easier for team members to pick up the phone and ask their coworkers for help even though they didn't work side by side.

I knew all too well that when you don't see someone regularly, they seem more like a stranger. And when you work with strangers, you're a lot less likely to raise your hand and say, "I need help" or, "I don't know the answer. Do you?" I also knew from years of volunteering that it's a lot easier to convince people to go that extra mile when they feel like they're doing it for a friend.

My least favorite moments came when I was faced with maneuvering the company through one of its employees' life events without feeling like an unempathetic corporate robot. Coming to the table to meet someone suffering from addiction, struggling with mental health conditions, or going through loss and grief, all while keeping the overall health of the company in mind, was one of the most difficult balancing acts I have ever experienced. It was gut-wrenching to step up as an amateur therapist while placing someone on a performance improvement plan, or worse, letting them go.

Aside from the responsibilities, some of the biggest challenges and moments of growth for me as a leader came from moments of political and social unrest. These life lessons opened my eyes to the inequality that still lives today. When George Floyd was murdered in May 2020, I was uncertain how to show up for our team members as they mourned. So I asked. Not knowing if by asking I would be insensitive to the situation, but knowing that I shouldn't ignore my ignorance, I carefully and thoughtfully asked how to provide support.

Then, when the COVID pandemic hit, I was tasked with creating processes and guiding our teams through building shutdowns, social distancing, cleaning protocols, and air-cleansing options. Even with all of the uncertainty surrounding me, I could have never expected the question my team members, who were people of color, asked:

"When we travel to a building at night, how do we convince a police officer we're supposed to be there?"

Employees often needed to travel for emergencies, but this went against lockdown restrictions, and the Black coworkers on my team were genuinely afraid about what could happen to them. I was floored. And I had no idea what to do in this situation, as it had never occurred to me that this could be an issue. My privilege was showing in a big way. So, I asked. I engaged in open dialogue, asking my team members directly about their needs and concerns so we could do everything possible to ensure their safety.

Life lessons and leadership lessons have blended for me many times. I didn't innately possess the ability to ask questions at the right times; I learned it from experience and hard knocks. In fact, one time when I didn't ask enough questions or the right questions, I got one of the biggest blended lessons of my life.

I accepted a job that promised to be a step up in my career—the first of my executive roles. I jumped on it, thinking that this kind of opportunity was few and far between. I thought, *If I don't take this now, I may not get another chance.* Ultimately, I took it without doing due diligence on the people I would be working with directly.

Of course I'd met those individuals during the course of interviewing, but I hadn't dug too deeply. I hadn't reached out to trusted sources and confirmed that we shared a vision or that our approaches were complementary. Instead, I'd taken the few meetings we had together at face value. During those meetings, I'd been greeted by charismatic and charming people who seemed to share my sentiment that things don't always have to be done the same way just because that's how they've worked before. We'd made a genuine connection, I felt.

When I accepted the role as Director of Property Management, I was elated and, head in the clouds, took a giant leap forward with my eyes shut.

The gig was overwhelming at times, but by and large tremendous. I was given free rein to make changes and right the ship. For a moment I felt unstoppable, as if I was coming into my own and had found my home. They even welcomed my quirky New Age thinking there. I could get the job done but also invite self-care back into my life. I was finally in a place where eyebrows didn't raise in disapproval when I would stop to meditate or ask if others wanted to join.

Then, somewhere between outrageous building emergencies, unreasonable client expectations, family ties that clouded judgment at how buildings should be managed, and the typical ebb and flow of managing people, I started noticing changes at the top. The charisma and charm that I'd initially found appealing started to shift. And the encouragement to let my freak flag fly started to feel more like a requirement of the job with rules, directions, and guardrails.

I eventually discovered that within the top leadership of the company, the primary person I was working with was a narcissist, and I didn't have the knowledge, tools, and skills to work with that personality type. I took one unsteady step after the next, figuring it out as I went. And I didn't always make great decisions. I've since learned that narcissists come in many shapes and sizes, but they have two things in common: an unreasonably high sense of self-importance and a dislike of criticism, even if it comes from a voice of reason.

Being a quick study, and bringing childhood lessons to the table for how to be the person someone needed me to be, I figured out that this person liked to be revered, and I found it relatively easy to cater to that need. I've since learned this isn't healthy or sustainable. But at that moment, all I knew was that they wanted to be loved and admired as a visionary. So, I placated them in multiple situations, until the admiration they so desired started shifting toward slanted ideals based on forced spirituality, and they started considering employees to be pseudo disciples.

Then the job started morphing and moving faster than even this talented shapeshifter could manage. From there, the demands got increasingly weirder. From company meetings turning into one-man shows about the power of the mind to hours-long one-on-one meetings that lost sight of any real business-directed agenda, this individual's needs and impulses took center stage even more of the time. They made bizarre requests to add diamond-like filters to buildings' water systems. They told us to overlook how family members ran questionable books. And they made reading about meritocracy mandatory.

My inner cheerleader and desire to champion all company initiatives were waning. Forcing ideas on employees and trying to mix spiritual growth with hard-and-fast financial duties was too much even for me. And yet, mixed in with the bizarre was a lot of good. There were incredible community-building, team-building, and self-building efforts, and we accomplished some big hairy goals.

Navigating the whims of the company's top leaders, particularly the lead I primarily reported to, was like playing hopscotch in the rain. You'd think that chalk-lined box would be in the same place as you hopped toward it, only to discover that it had been washed away, with only a blurred sketch left. It was nearly impossible to gauge whether the company was outlandish or brilliantly different. Regardless, the roller coaster became exhausting, and my once polite patience for meeting agendas far removed from the business that I would be forced to make up for at night, started to fade.

A big turning point came during the planning of a half-day retreat. The company's leaders disregarded reasonable preparations for time away from the office and away from fiduciary duties. I desperately tried to present ideas I thought were based on common sense and common courtesy, but they ignored them. They lacked interest in compromise at this moment, instead indicating that I wasn't adapting quickly enough. All of this culminated in a surreal situation. My team and I found ourselves seated in an auditorium, all emergency phones save one (mine) turned off, listening to a spiritual leader guide us through meditation and a contemplation of different ways to approach problems. If I hadn't been forced to do this, or it hadn't been the middle of a workday, I might have been open-minded enough to try and learn something.

The final straw came when I went head-to-head with the company's leaders in the argument of my career. One thing to note is that handling contracts in the property management world eventually becomes second nature to any seasoned manager. So when the company decided to renegotiate the employee contracts, the employees went through them with a fine-toothed comb. And they found that the contracts were riddled with inconsistencies and clauses that I wouldn't have wished on anyone. I started fielding calls from team members, who asked in exasperation, "Have you read this?" Since I hadn't been given the opportunity to read the document before it went out, I wasn't prepared to answer. However, it didn't take long for me to realize that the well-being of those I led was at stake, so I went to battle for them.

In the end, I lost more than the battle. I lost the war. I walked away from the role that I'd so eagerly taken. It was a painful loss that included leaving behind relationships I'd carefully created, for having contact with me would have led to negative repercussions for those people. I was grateful that I could walk away from a contract that I considered to be a detriment to my fair employment, but I still felt like a failure.

I couldn't figure out how things had gone south so fast. I didn't understand how I'd missed the early signs that would have deterred me from taking the job to begin with. And for fuck's sake, with all the meditating and quiet contemplation, how had I allowed myself to get swept up? How had I gotten pushed into cheerleading for someone who didn't deserve my enthusiasm or support?

Upon someone's suggestion, I started reading about narcissism. In doing so, I learned that checking your ego at the door is paramount to maintaining a relationship with a narcissist. I also discovered that going to battle is a waste of energy. While that might be true, it sure as shit didn't sit well with me. Sometimes going to battle is necessary. And that's when I stopped beating myself up over someone else's attempt to manipulate me.

I had to be pushed to realize my worth, and to understand that sometimes speaking up or walking out *is* the right answer. Being complicit, bullied, or silenced in that situation was no longer an option. The experience reminded me that leading is so much harder than managing. When you lead, you care about the people around you. You're willing to walk away from a job you love to prove that everyone you lead is worth listening to.

Picking up my "Good Things Come to Those Who Work Their Asses Off" notebook once again, I dusted myself off and proceeded to move forward with my newfound skills to ask the right questions, speak up, and walk out when necessary.

Your Turn

If you're lucky enough to find yourself in a position to lead others, I hope you'll ask yourself, "What kind of leader do I choose to be today?" Regardless of *who* you lead—coworkers, sports teams, volunteers, children—the intention behind *how* you lead is paramount. I believe that begins with awareness and purposefully setting an intention. In my opinion it's the first step in what separates a manager from a leader. In fact, I believe the delineation of managers versus leaders is relatively simple. Managers show up, ensure others show up, and get the work produced. Leaders guide and champion the people on their teams. They take time to coach even when time is limited. They trust and empower others to step up while allowing space for mistakes that happen. They offer judgment-free zones for mistakes because they understand that with the right conversations and coaching, a large amount of individual and family, school, team, or company growth can come from those mistakes. And finally, they aren't afraid to ask when they don't know the answer. Better yet, they hire for their personal gaps in knowledge and learn from those around them.

One of the biggest lessons I had to learn in a leadership position was listening to my intuition. I had to learn that when something didn't feel right, it was okay to give that feeling space and then act on it with the current data I had and the data I'd collected over many years of trial and error.

As you step into your leadership roles, what do you hope to bring to the table? How do you hope to shape the lives of those you lead?

The unspoken energy that draws you in, that leads you to turn left instead of right, is there at all times. It's at the center of your being.

When you close your eyes and tell the noise to step aside, you can feel it—sense it—and hear it.

This is your intuition. And it's never wrong.

Alchemized Woman

CHAPTER THIRTEEN

The fear of completing this book is sinking its grubby claws into my chest. What lies beyond this final chapter? Does finishing this work signal that I've somehow figured out life? Has stepping through the looking glass to reflect on my life's work toward growth been enough to help me understand who I am today? The unknown feels daunting. And although fear is attempting to bring me to a screeching halt, I refuse to yield to its pressure.

Stripped of my roles, masks, and titles, who am I as a woman, an individual, a human? Without those definitions, who are any of us? I often find myself grappling with this question as I continue to search for meaning in life. Meaning, after all, is what gives us purpose, power, and the motivation we need to keep moving forward when shit gets dark. It gives us the strength we need to shine through the storm. Though my journey is ongoing, and it may take a lifetime to answer the question of meaning, I have discovered a few insights in addition to the ones I've already shared.

I am a woman who encompasses both feminine and masculine energy. It is woven into my fabric, as it's woven into every fiber of our energetically connected world. A part of that connection, I embody my role in our collective experience.

And while I acknowledge that scars can limit one's ability to trust, I choose to rediscover new and meaningful connections despite the pain of past experiences.

Drawing upon resilience with relative ease, I can find the gumption to pick myself up, dust myself off, and try again after falling or being knocked down. However, I also know I don't always have to do it alone. I now fully understand and appreciate the power of friendship, teamwork, and community. I have witnessed the strength that comes from supporting each other and finding joy in the small moments when faced with adversity or chaos. And I no longer take for granted the collective strength that emerges when motivated individuals come together.

Adaptation and the willingness to change remain an essential part of who I am. I have learned through adversity how to turn challenges into opportunities for growth. But now, comfortable with who I am at my core, I remain open to challenging myself to be better without the need for another's approval. Still, I know I can't always see the forest for the trees, so with an open heart, I remain diligent in my watchfulness for and ability to welcome angels who offer guidance right when I need it most.

I remain steadfast in my quest for mindfulness, knowing full well that the sensations and cues my body sends out are what alert me to the spaces within me that need attention. Following them like clues to the deeper meaning they serve, those physical sensations center me in the importance of interconnected physical, mental, and emotional well-being. From that centered place, I find courage and power. It allows me the ability to tap into vulnerable places and expose them to the world as I reach for those moments when others can see the real me—the me who possesses the power to transform painful memories into compassion for myself and others. The me who trusts that our vulnerability is what leads us to true connection. And it's our vulnerability that brings forgiveness to light.

I'm a woman who makes mistakes and is grateful for the forgiveness I've been granted. Once a happy-go-lucky girl who put a positive spin on everything, now I am a woman who embraces the many layers that make me human. I can hold space for the light and the shadow within me. I no longer feel the need to push the darkness that's begging to be seen under the covers. Instead, I hold it tight and honor that it is a part of me.

I am a "woo" woman, a star child born into this world with a mission to expand as a being of light and to help others do the same. I know that when we each breathe, so does the world. That's just how connected we all are.

I am balanced, then unbalanced, and then balanced once again. I respect the seesaw that is life—the ebb and flow of occurrences that push or pull us through our days. At times we feel our feet firmly planted on the ground beneath us, and at others we dangle from above, hoping to find our footing again soon. When confronted by the complexities of balancing well-being, my higher self, ego, expectations, boundaries, and all the parts of life that get thrown at my feet, I trust my intuition to help guide me back toward my authentic center. For in that center lies the essence of who I am—a woman continually unfolding, learning, and evolving.

Your Turn

My strength, found in a connection to the energy that threads us together in our collective human experience, is bolstered when I breathe. This is true for each of us. I learned this from a vision I had a few years ago: a tiny blue-and-green bird sitting on the top rail of a dining chair at a small wooden kitchen table. With each breath the bird took, its chest expanded—feathers unfolding to invite space for its inhalation. On the table sat a globe, and with each breath the bird took, the globe expanded as well.

When we each breathe, the whole world feels it. When we each heal, speak with kindness, allow love to win, and lead with compassion, the whole world feels it. For we are like a grove of aspen trees. Our energetic root system connects us all together, to the earth, and to the Universe. Whatever phase of life you find yourself in, whether you've fallen or you're just beginning to rise, whether you lead others in a dance or choose to be a backup dancer, the time to remember your roots is now. The energy beckons; it welcomes you to tap in and become rooted. Although this force cannot be seen by the naked eye, it can be felt, and it can refuel us, rebalance us, energize us, and remind us of who we are. Sink into its embrace. Imagine roots growing from your feet and your spine into the earth and branching out to connect with all those around you. I'll be there waiting for you, because I am a part of this energetic system. We all are.

As elusive and imperfect as it may be, balance is here for you now. Reach for it. Love however it shows up for you at this moment.

Breathe.

Now invite others to join you. Show up as imperfect and unpolished—and allow them to do the same. Your kindness, your vulnerability, is all we need. It's enough.

You are enough.

Acknowledgments

Writing this book was a project like none other I've ever faced. And while the first draft poured out of me faster than Coke from a shook-up bottle, the drafts that followed took effort, commitment, and at times, a real team effort. To these people who helped me find my courage, words, and confidence: I will be forever grateful.

My Editor

Elena Vega: Thank you so much for helping make sense of my thoughts and for helping to pull together the final pieces of this book. Your words of encouragement and your guidance on how to proceed have helped me immensely. I am so very thankful for all of your help. www.elenavegawordpro.com

My Cover Designer

Annemarie Lamprecht: I feel so lucky to have found you. Thank you so much for helping breathe color and life into the book through your incredible design. www.anibuchner.myportfolio.com

My Therapist

Jenny Bierman: Your patience and guidance in helping me work through some of the jarring and painful memories in order to heal and to write this book have forever changed me. Thank you so much for helping me get through the tough shit.

My BLT

For all of my friends who jumped in early to join my Book Launch Team: your help with launching this book is hard to measure and why would I even try!? Thank you so much for taking the time to read updates, weigh in on decisions, and get the word out. Without you this thing may never have made it out of Colorado. Thank you!

My Soul Family

Love and so much gratitude to Mama, Dad, and Audel Cayce for reading, encouraging, and offering me peace when I needed it.

Thank you Grace and Johnny Didway, for taking me in when you didn't have to, for sharing your wisdom, and for helping me become the woman I am today.

To Mel and Jen, how could I ever begin to thank y'all for all of the support you consistently show? Your unconditional friendship and love is more than this girl could ever have asked for. Thank you for being my first wives club. Love ya both more than my luggage.

Mike, there just aren't enough words. Between the encouragement to go to Sedona, your steadfast support when the hardest memories came forth, and your undying love through all the thick and thin we've faced, I just don't know how I could ever truly thank you. My heart is full. LYSM

Notes

CHAPTER THREE: Dance Team Captain
Reference "Oh buy my darling, what if you fly?" is by Erin Hanson, *"The Poetic Underground #2, Voyage"*

CHAPTER FIVE: Survivor
EMDR—Eye Movement Desensitization and Reprocessing—www.emdr.com

WHAT HAPPENED TO YOU: Conversations on Trauma, Resilience, and Healing, by Oprah Winfrey and Dr. Bruce Perry, MD, Ph.D.

CHAPTER NINE: Wife
"Two Become One"—In online research, it seems this quote may be referenced in multiple sections, translations, and/or editions of the Bible.

CHAPTER TWELVE: Executive
"Good things come to those who work their asses off"—It is unknown who originally coined this quote; however, it was used in the 2014 movie *Nightcrawler* written by screenwriter, Daniel Christopher Gilroy.

About The Author

Brandi Herdzina is a motivational speaker, coach, and the author of *Shine Through The Storm: Inspirational Stories to Discover Inner Strength and Balance*. A Jill of all trades, she found her rhythm in commercial real estate for twenty years, then decided to return to her purpose. Now she works with teams, associations, and individuals to help bring people together, empower leaders, and guide seekers to rediscover balance and passion for life. Brandi lives in Colorado with her husband and their dog (a "chatty pappy"), Finnley. When she isn't working, she's spending time with her family and friends, traveling, cooking, reading, watching binge-worthy TV, painting (poorly), or hiking.

www.ingramcontent.com/pod-product-compliance
Lightning Source LLC
Chambersburg PA
CBHW070703130626
46553CB00005B/1813